Does Your Meter Work?!

A Gift For:

From:

Does Your Meter Work?!

Published by:

Western Publishing
Box 41
Edmonton, Alberta, Canada
T5J 2G9

Cover photography by Dr. Ross Danyluk and Jim Soliski
Cover design by Tammy Lee Valgardson and Jim Soliski

Printed in Canada

National Library of Canada Cataloguing in Publication

Soliski, Jim, 1961-
    Does your meter work?! / Jim Soliski.

ISBN 0-9734809-0-4

    1.Soliski, Jim, 1961- --Travel. 2.Voyages
and travels. 3.Asia--Description and travel.
I.Title.

    DS10.S64 2004   910.4   C2004-900827-7

Does Your Meter Work?!

To Dragana,
Because 25 years ago you saw this book before anyone…

Does Your Meter Work?!

Does Your Meter Work?!

Travel ought to be fun, and so should reading about it. Few travel writers have more fun than Jim Soliski – and it shows in his writing.
Randy Curwen, Chicago Tribune

Forget fluffy clouds and turquoise seas: Jim Soliski writes real travel. Fast-paced, punchy and often very funny, this is the man to read if you know what travel is.
Jack Barker, Travelmag.co.uk

When I get a fresh story, I normally switch to hard-ass mode, combing the copy for holes, errors and leaps of logic. But I've found that damn hard to do with Jim Soliski's travel pieces because he ventures to such interesting--and, often, personally dangerous--places, and paints such vivid pictures with his words…he sucks me into his overseas tales…which means I have to go back and give his copy hard reads again in search of holes, errors and leaps of logic (thankfully, they're few and far between). So I'd like to take this opportunity to chastise Mr. Soliski for all the extra work he's heaped on me over the years--and thank him for all the good reads.
Matt Coker, Orange County Weekly

In an age where every second counts, Jim Soliski is one 'guide' who can show you the world - and still get you home in time for supper, albeit wide-eyed and brimming with excitement from your travels.
Mike Gillespie, Ottawa Citizen

I can read Jim Soliski with confidence the result will be both delightful and shocking.
Harriet Heithaus, Naples Daily News

"…so glib that he even fooled me into buying his stuff…"
Bob Jenkins, St. Petersburg Times

Always a pearl among the turds.
Alan Kerr, Providence Journal

Does Your Meter Work?!

Some guys are tourists and some guys are travellers. And then there's Soliski, a guy with a penchant for finding a good yarn in the unlikeliest of places.
Paul Waters, Montreal Gazette

It's easy to get caught up in the seemingly unbelievable tales of Filipino fighting chickens, sadistic ticket agents in India, and re-entry culture shock. In Does Your Meter Work, Soliski figuratively dodges those familiar bullets often aimed at solo travellers as he takes us around the world, one mishap at a time. His frenetic, fly by the seat of his pants approach to travel is like his writing, it's never dull.
Kisha Ferguson, Outpost Magazine Co-founder,
Writer/Broadcaster

I wouldn't necessarily want to actually travel WITH Jim Soliski - too many brushes with hostile local authorities and dangerous forms of local transportation for my taste. But I'm glad that through his funny, descriptive writing, he has taken me along for the ride anyway.
Patricia Rodriguez, Fort Worth Star-Telegram

It is said chuckling is good for us because it massages our inner organs. If that is so, then Jim Soliski's travel anecdotes should be required reading on a daily basis. His travel escapades and unique view of the world will have you chuckling for hours.
Donna Vieira, DreamScapes Travel & Lifestyle Magazine

Like any good travel writer who moonlights as a cab driver, Jim Soliski has a trunk full of stories and a critical eye. His trenchant and slightly askew observations on the vagaries of touring in distant lands are akin to the discovery that the food you're eating isn't the innocuous meal you expected. The flavours, texture and contents are unique, interesting and maybe a little scary.
Chris Allen, CKUA Radio Network

Does Your Meter Work?!

Jim Soliski´s travel adventures have traversed the web pages of www.babylontravel.net for the past 5 years bringing a vibrant and honest glimpse of the world the way Jim sees it. Jim has inspired all of us at Babylon Travel with his passion for travel and his never-ending wit.
Lisa Ismael, BabylonTravel.net

What separates Jim Soliski from other travel writers is the way he focuses on the unexpected, offbeat moments he's experienced in his wide-ranging travels, putting them at the centre of his compulsively readable stories. Whether it's the pitfalls of rafting in Nepal, haggling over train tickets with an inflexible bureaucrat in India, or hitching his way across Malaysia in a gazillion different vehicles, Soliski doesn't shy away from adventure, big or small -- he dives into it headlong. He's also got a great ear for dialogue, which he uses to terrific effect in the title story of this collection.
Stephen Whitworth, prairie dog magazine

Hits your funny bone time and again with great little insights into backpacker travels.
Babak Fakhamzadeh, Travelhog.net

Only someone with Jim's genuine sense of adventure can communicate the joy of exploring the familiar and the exotic.
Kevin Wilson, SEE Magazine

Does Your Meter Work?!

Does Your Meter Work?!

It is as clear to me as sunshine that the greatest possible stumbling blocks in the path of human happiness and improvements are these heaps of bricks and stones, consolidated with mortar, or hewn timber, fastened together with spike nails, which men painfully contrive for their own torment, and call them house and home! The soul needs air; a wide sweep and frequent change of it.

Nathaniel Hawthorne

Foreword

So you want to be a writer, huh? I had always fancied the idea, but earlier in life, writing was impossible because there was always another weekend tournament, another cover charge to pay, another fox telling me that she was washing her hair: in other words, I was too busy being twentysomething. Still the thought of writing hectored away inside me.

Running both ways at once, I scraped out a degree in English Lit. Typical comments on my assignments went like this: "Serious misunderstanding of Shakespeare/Austen/Hawthorne/Hemingway, but a lively read. Five out of nine."

After university, I began to travel. I wrote nothing but letters home, and I always thought my friends were kidding when they said that they still kept and reread my letters. The kicker to begin writing came during a plane ride seated beside a cool Kiwi on the Brisbane-Auckland leg of a Christchurch-bound milk run. During a lull in the conversation, he asked, "So…are you a writer?" "No." "Oh … you seem like a writer." What did that mean? Maybe I really should try.

After Christchurch, I left on a solo trip across Asia: the writing bug was in full jailbreak. Short stories? Poetry? How about a travel book? I'll be the first, for sure. About a week into the trip, after umpteen laps around my Filipino beach hut mumbling, "Write the first word and you can never go back. Will you see it through?," I wrote the first word. The genie and her bottle had parted for good.

Asia turned out to be a busy place for a man trying to find a career while en route to somewhere as yet undetermined. There were the cockfights in the Philippines, scuba diving in the South China Sea, a climb up the tallest peak in South East Asia, hitchhiking from Brunei to Bangkok, the Khmer Rouge and the ineluctable Angkor Wat in Cambodia, then a short stint teaching English in frenetic Saigon. As I traveled through Vietnam on my way out of the country, an exquisite local lady and I fell head over tea kettle in love, and we lived a lifetime in a matter of eleven days. She was worth every word of our unavoidable parting.

There was more than love out there. Tiger Woods winning the Master's on tape delay in a chicken joint in Laos, white-water rafting in the Himalayas, Hindu blessings at sunrise on The Ganges River, the Indian train system, border troubles, elephant rides, and automatic weapons up my snoot in Sri Lanka. Then, after two years and 25,000 miles, there was the cold, wet fish in the face of the order, quiet, and personal space of North America.

Heaps of material to write about.

After I arrived home in Canada, I took a walk through my local bookstore where I asked about travel books. The clerk must have shown me a hundred of them. Maybe a hundred and a half. I was in trouble.

Day after day during the week I wrote and rewrote on a dinosaur of a word processor. Taxi driving on the weekends, editing hard copy between fares. My friends asked, "Why don't you get a job?" My mother never asked a thing.

Finally, I had a glistening manuscript. One so full of wit and savvy, I'd need to take my laundry basket to the mailbox to lug home the offers. Using the *Writer's Market* reference book, I spent a king's ransom on mail-outs. Form letters from publishers inside my self addressed stamped envelopes arrived furiously: *"Dear Author, Thank you for thinking of us, but we don't see a fit with our list for this year, or the future. Good luck in placing your work."*

Dead already and forever. I recalled the old joke: A boy was playing in a band at half time of a football game. After the performance, his father hugs him and says, "Son, I'm proud of you. Everyone was out of step out there except you!"

Travel had started me on the writer's path, so I journeyed to New York to visit a friend and hawk my manuscript to the Big Apple's hawks. However, a dove of an editor inadvertently provided me with my turning point. She asked if I'd been published before. "Nowhere? Maybe you should try to get some stories in the magazines."

I returned home and mined a list of editors from the library, investing another fortune in photocopies and stamps for cold submissions to publications large and small, known and not. I rarely heard back from anyone, even though I always included a self-addressed stamped envelope.

One of the few to respond came from The LA Times Syndicate about my cockfight story: scrawled in the margin, *"No thanks. Who would want to read this piece anyways?"* Oddly, the next week, The Seattle Times wrote back on the same story: *"Thanks, but I'll pass. Nice description, however. Pictures so so."* Two editors had found the time to comment. Was this luck, or misfortune? Or both: any news was better than no news. The next month, Harper's, the well-known publication, did a 4000-word expose on cockfighting in the American south. It wasn't Asia, but feeling vindicated, I photocopied the cover page of Harper's, the copy of my story, and mailed the package to the LA Times editor with a note that read, simply, "Harper's!"

With that bridge burnt, the next line of attack on the publishing world was to use the newest road, e-mail. I found a site, www.usnewspaperlinks.com that had links to nearly every newspaper in America. I chose the person most likely to bite and pitched my Asia writings to each paper, personalizing my killer one-page query letter and buff About The Author. The number of e-mails I sent off was literally in the thousands. I was impressed; not everyone else was:

Dear Mr. Soliski:

No thanks. Also, in the future, you should probably not address persons you do not know by their first names. That's a habit of our generation I do not like, and I don't appreciate it, although having read as much of your hip autobiography as I could without getting sick, I would expect it. Anyway, I think I'll pass.

Regards,
R. Cort Kirkwood

Dear Jim, in the future you should ask the publication if they are interested in your work before sending it. I may have to bill you the time it took to download them and put them in the trash. We are a small publication only interested in news generated within or about people resideing (sic) in our boundaries. My business manager makes me account for ever (sic) minute of my time and unfortunately, you just used many of them. Please remove us from your mass mailing.
Sincerely, Bonnie MacNeill, managing editor

Dear Jim,

I don't appreciate form-letter resumes sent in the guise of personal letters. In fact, they really piss me off. If you want to write for my newspaper, tell me why my newspaper in particular. But don't bother with us, you've already blown it. I'm just giving you advice for future cold-call attempts.
Sincerely,
Matt Taibbi

Most folks in the business were, at worst, benign:

"Jim, thanks for your note. I'm not looking to add a free-lance writer's submissions to our lifestyle section at this time. Good luck. Chris

Jim, Thanks for the message and for the way in which you outlined the articles you would like to offer. Very effective. I have forwarded your message to our Lifestyles editor, Jennifer Becknell, but I must tell you we don't buy much freelance. What we do buy in travel usually are done by local folks. Our focus is very much on our circulation area. Terry Plumb, editor

Intimidated as hell by the e-mail exchanges, I took a deep breath and picked up the phone, but editors were far too busy to hear from, and to take seriously, a writer without credits. Then, another turning point. Transitions Abroad, a pithy magazine from Massachusetts agreed to print my story about how to go overseas to teach English. Finally, I had a credit. And a check for $35 US dollars. That was the beginning. From that moment, conversations with editors changed immediately when they heard "yes" to their question, "Have you been published before?" Buoyed with enthusiasm, I marched on with my reinforced pitch:

Jim:
Quite the intro letter. Though I could guess, I need to ask: Was any of your travel subsidized by any destination or travel seller? If not, howsabout sending me Not my war and Knights in feathered armor, to eyeball? I'll get back to you within a week of receiving them.
Bob Jenkins
Travel Editor
Petersburg Times

Bob (one of Earth's funniest guys) bought Knights in Feathered Armor aka poor chickens in cockfights and another four stories since. Also:

Received your fascinating photo essay. Tell me what your price is, while I ask our graphics editor what we can afford. Harriet Heithaus

Since some of the editors actually wrote to me, I knew I was on the correct path.

Submissions from hopeful, or hopeless, neophyte authors inundate editors. A response from the editor of a major U.S. newspaper, even if he doesn't buy, is a coup:

Can you tell us how you came to be traveling around Asia? Were these the result of sponsored trips in any way? --Howie Shapiro, Philadelphia Inquirer travel editor

Send me your single best story and we'll see. –Howie

Does Your Meter Work?!

There is no royal road to Philly, my Mr. Shapiro still hasn't taken one of my stories, but he answers all my queries, which says a lot to my eyes about how he feels about my writing. Sometimes there's nothing anyone with such feelings can do:

Jim,

As you know, I like your writing, but my budget is almost entirely earmarked for specific needs in special sections. So, I'll have to say no to this story and your other Borneo piece. Alan Kerr Providence Journal

Once stories have been published, disapproval comes with the territory. While the intention is not to upset your readers, you must be prepared to accept the lead flowers:

I read your article on cockfighting in the Phillipines (sic). Why did you write it? To tell all barbaric and violent people that there is a shameful country that allows this horrendous act for them to go to on vacation? Why didn't you mention how brutal it was? How barbaric it was? Your ending was sickening. "I wasn't in the mood for chicken"? Think of those poor roosters that died terribly or lingered in pain til they were killed. Next time write about someplace enjoyable to visit or at least point out the brutality of the acts taking place.

Also:

Globe and Mail adventure travel writer, Jim Soliski's article, Saturday, October 20, describing his first scuba dive after a five minute lesson in the Phillipine (sic) town of El Nido, flies in the face of what responsible scuba diving is all about.

A suggestion to dive in countries that need your money more than they need your admiration is an invitation to throw all caution to the wind.

Concern for liabilities and to promote a healthy respect for diving safety, responsible resorts offering scuba diving insist all non certified "wannabe divers" receive at the bare minimum a 30 minute resort or pool course prior to any attempt at an open water dive accompanied by a dive instructor, usually to a depth no deeper than 10 metres.

The underwater world is indeed a sight to behold. Jim Soliski's description of his first dive, included the dive masters handling of a so called inert dynamite stick, the dive master looking for him at a 20 metre depth and then ocean currents spiralling them to the surface terminating the dive prematurely, should lead any knowledgeable diver to suggest Jim was lucky to survive his first dive.

Writing as a certified diver, this article is not in my opinion representative of what responsible dive agencies, dive instructors and certified divers advocate.

Please let the diving world know where Mr. Soliski's next dive destination will be so that it can be avoided.

Gerry Wood
352 Glengarry Avenue
Toronto, Ontario,
905-678-6584

The most vitriolic criticism came after a story about Saigon prostitution that ran in an alternative weekly:

I think it's great that Vue Weekly is shrugging off political correctness and giving its readers the coverage they deserve of fun to be had with sex for sale in other countries. In "The Lay of the Land" Jim Soliski showed us how to get back at those pushy Saigon whores. I'm looking forward to more groundbreaking prostitution coverage in Vue – maybe Jim will turn his astute reporter's eye to those annoying yet innately sexy child prostitutes of Bangkok, or ways of getting back at workers in Edmonton's own fun, fun sex trade.

All right, enough of the sarcasm. I can't tell you how pissed off and disappointed I was finding "The Lay of the Land" in Vue. Jim Soliski comes across as a smug asshole with no awareness of the economic or gender issues that make prostitution such a complex issue. I don't believe you should publish the work of a travel reporter so manifestly ignorant of what it means to be a privileged Canadian romping through other people's countries and lives; his lack of insight and self-reflectiveness is just horrifying.

I usually pick Vue up before See because Vue comes across as the more intelligent and politically savvy of the two. Another couple of sexist, xenophobic, downright moronic articles by the likes of Soliski could certainly change my mind.

David Kahane, Department of Philosophy, University of Alberta

Mr. Kahane got his wish. My bi-weekly column that had run for a year lasted one more story, and I was punted from the payroll. But the publications have continued, the hate-mail smaller and milder, the editors had more of me on paper to read before they bought, The Alberta Foundation for the Arts gave me a tiny grant, and I was, well, a writer, almost ready to pay taxes…with a fan club of one:

Dear Jim Soliski,

What a descriptive and gifted writer you are! I have just finished reading your wonderful article on Angkor Wat, in Saturday's Vancouver Sun, and I'm ready to go to see this majestic place…

…This is a spot in the world I've always wanted to see and your article has assured me that I will be there soon. Thank you so much.

Sincerely, Hilde Abt

Nine months later a postcard from Angkor, complete with a Cambodian stamp, arrived:

Dear Jim,

Does Your Meter Work?!

Thanks to you, my husband & I made it to a "place to come & simply be." You are so right when you say that poets & historians have done their best to describe the splendour, but seeing it with your own eyes has been the ultimate! It is a spectacular architectural wonder, something we will never forget. Many thanks to you. Sincerely, Hilde Abt (Delta B.C.)

Now…give me a second…sniff…Hilde, while I collect myself…your two notes make the whole bloody thing worthwhile.

With over 170 credits to date, the writing world has sometimes been funny as well as frightening. Believe it or not, I've sold:

- The same story to the same paper twice (the editor was aware)

- Stories to the same editor who had rejected it earlier (they either forgot they read the piece, or more likely, never read it in the first place)

- The same stories to archrival newspapers. (An accident. By the time I realized the second story ran, it was too late. So I held my breath for the sky to fall, but it didn't.)

- The cockfight story around ten times, and no one has picketed my home or goose blind yet.

What have I learned from this trip through the wonderland of magazine and newspaper publishing?

- Swallow your pride, get e-mail, run up a huge phone bill without wavering, and keep replying no matter what they say to you.

- As kind as most editors are, they are often equally hesitant about putting their boss's fortune at your disposal. Their motto is "I'll Take A Chance On You If Someone Did Before Me."

- Promises are made to be broken on the editor's side, not yours, and the editor owes it to his boss over you. Back to the phones, letters, and e-mails.

Does Your Meter Work?!

- Editors don't return messages, so keep calling back. They have to be in their offices at some point. If the phone picks up right away, they're on the other line, and that's your cue to call back often, as in redial immediately. Patience counts, decorum be damned.

- The paper business is capricious. News changes in real time, which will work for and against you.

- The most important tool in a writer's box is to have something to say. After that, luck plays a big part because getting published relies so much on the right piece in the right hands at the right time.

- Write because you want to. The percentage of writers who make their sole living from writing is small.

- Get a personal "editor," a freebie who's reliable, keen, on your side, and unafraid to debate you. Two is better. I have five friends who always edit for me. I wish I had ten.

- Establish a beachhead. Anything published anywhere at any price, including free stuff appearing in a free magazine, has value in your resume. Success in getting yourself published is infinitely more difficult without some sort of track record. A major magazine wrote back:

hi jim,
honestly, i would normally not reply to the kind of query you sent us (impersonal, broadcast, general, etc.), but as you've been published in a couple of reputable places and have been traveling quite a bit, we might be able to work something out.

Nothing has worked out with that editor so far, but life, like travel, is a journey, not a destination. Oh, and avoid clichés like the plague. Everything you write can fit somewhere, some time -- just keep looking and writing. Calling, too. You'll end up "able to work something out."

Does Your Meter Work?!

Remember that glistening manuscript? Armed with 170 stories published, and the knowledge that 60 or so professional newspaper and magazine editors along the way deemed that my stuff was worth their money, I queried the agents. Over a hundred. Eight asked for sample chapters…not one asked to see more. Back to the publishers. Fifty-five queries, four asked for samples…no takers.

Finally, my battered ego forced a board meeting with the chief shareholder of the Jim Soliski Benevolent Fund. We concluded that the horizon held little hope of the manuscript's viability as a commercial product. That's delicate code for, "The book's not good enough."

Hence, this book, a self-published anthology of the stories that were good enough for the likes of the Chicago Tribune, Boston Globe, San Francisco Examiner, The St. Petersburg Times, The Naples Daily News, Travelers' Tales, OC Weekly (Anaheim's Village Voice), The Georgia Strait, Outpost Magazine, most of the major papers in Canada, and so on. Even publications in Britain, Hong Kong, and Peru. Some of the stories herein have yet to fool any editors, so, dear reader, humor me as I impose them on you.

In that spirit, I hope you enjoy reading my stories as much as I've adored living then writing them. Please look for pictures on the web site: www.doesyourmeterwork.com.

Jim Soliski

…but first, I need to thank a few folks because one person doth not a book wrought. I'll begin with my English professor troika for the epiphanies they supplied. Drs. Dale Wilkie, Eileen Conway, and Bob Solomon. Dr. Bob, a great friend, your guidance, firmness, gentleness, and impeccable edits grant you huge sweat equity in DYMW, and thanks for fixing my &#^% computer all those times. Dr. Ross Danyluk, Mr. Joe Murray, Mr. Weston Benjamin, Mr. Derek Nile, your edits, comments, and support have been above the call. Web guru Mr. Roland Popadynetz, and a real friend and supporter since we were wee gaffers, thank you. Drs. Tissa and

Does Your Meter Work?!

Mary Kappagoda, mentors and inspirations. To my family of friends who are still my friends, well, I guess I could've got a job but this book was in the way…

Does Your Meter Work?!

Does Your Meter Work?!

Does Your Meter Work?!

DOES YOUR METER WORK?!

"Does your meter work?!"

"No, sir."

Next cab.

"Does your meter work?!"

"No, sir."

Next cab.

"Does your meter work?!"

"No, sir."

No taxi driver wants to use his meter because some charitable government officials, who probably have a few cousins in the business, had established overblown fixed rates from the Manila airport to the various parts of the city - in the $15 to $20 range. One company controlled a monopoly in the departures area. I was asking in the arrivals. Any driver can bring trips to the airport and I wanted an independent operator. Next cab.

"Does your meter work?!"

No verbal response, just a tough-guy Clint Eastwood type of nod. I hopped in and we took off and down the ramp. Once we were under way, he still hadn't started his meter.

"Could you please turn your meter on."

He leaned to his right, unlatched the glove compartment, and calmly fished around. His fingers gripped something (I held my breath for the pistola) and came up with an imitation leather-clad book containing a jumble of papers with the apparent "official" rates inscribed on record.

"This is my meter."

"Turn your meter on or let me out!"

Muttering four-letter words in Tagalog, the language of the Philippines, he agreed. The rear passenger doors of Filipino taxis are rigged to a handle beside the driver. My presumed cabby-du-jour hammered the brakes, popped the door open, and silently looked over his right shoulder in unspoken solicitation for my feet to reacquaint themselves with the dusty concrete road.

Pulling the door shut, he made a U-turn in pursuit of inflated fare. I was satisfied; we had traveled far enough away from the terminal for me to flag down another taxi. Anyone coming along empty would be not one of the official bandits, but an also-ran of the Manila taxi fiefdom deadheading out and, naturally, looking for flags. I waved another cab down without delay.

"Does your meter work?" I wanted to know.

"Yes, sir."

"Will you use it?"

"Yes, yes, no problem."

I vaulted in and we peeled away.

"Where do you want to go, sir?"

"I want to go to Manila, Mabini Street."

"Yes, sir, Mabini Street."

We bumped along through some construction detours.

"Where are you from, sir?" he wanted to know.

"I'm from Canada. Can you turn your meter on?"

"Yes sir. From Canada. I have a cousin in Toronto."

Everyone I ever met in Asia had a cousin in Toronto.

"You pay extra for air-con, okay?" he continued.

"Pay extra for air-con?"

"Yes sir, surcharge."

"How much is air-con surcharge?"

"Five dollars U.S."

"What if you turn off the air-con and I just roll the window down?"

"No, no, sir, we cannot do that."

We turned onto a busy road. A taxi was parked against the curb.

"I'm not paying for air-con. Let me out - here, here is another taxi parked. Stop! STOP!"

Without a word, the cabby opened and closed my door and drove off into that carnage called traffic. I looked around for the possible maestro of this new, potential ride. The car didn't appear damaged or look abandoned; in fact, it was running. Twenty yards away, facing a busted-up fence, a guy was taking a leak. Twisting to see me representing hard currency, he popped junior back into his hiding place and sprinted over with a radioactive smile. His meter worked, his air-con didn't; I arrived on Mabini Street right on schedule and budget - under three dollars.

That morning was my release date from an eight-month sentence of teaching English in Taiwan where, this time, I had managed to save just under $11,000. I only knew a few things.

Does Your Meter Work?!

First, I wanted to travel "à la carte"; there was no set menu. Each destination would be an item of my choosing. There would be no deadlines or bosses; no one calling me, needing me, or counting my money. Second, I sweated for that money and I wanted maximum bang for minimum buck. Third, I knew that whatever was in store, it was going to be good. Let's go.

UNEARTH YOU TRAVELING À LA CARTE

Enduring long rides from a constellation of transportation modes, from train to plane and footsmobile to yak, comes with the territory of traveling à la carte. One night, while on an overnight ferry, the only lights were sparsely peppered on the shores of Luzon - the Philippines' biggest island - and the stars. The half moon wore a charcoal gray ring when it occasionally grappled out from behind a cloud.

Often the scuttle that travelers report is the cliché "finding oneself." With nothing but time in abundance, you're free of distractions: no family members down your back, no upset customer to face tomorrow, no office politics to contend with, no overdue utility bills. Consequently, the mind becomes uncluttered, clearing the way for profound levels of thought and reflection. With you providing all the dialogue, clear, full, intimate conversations are possible with a sibling concerning something that happened among you two as children. Recall is like real time to discuss the occurrence's ramifications, contribute personal insights, explain why it had to happen, and eventually find the elusive closure that had been swimming in the unconscious until now, docking at the wharf of your inner peace.

The same holds true with perhaps a full discussion with a close friend whose spouse inexplicably left, the answer to why is still a mystery until now, when you, and the friend in absentia, each have reached the same conclusion in your mind. Hopefully, your new found enlightenment can be gifted to him at an appropriate time.

"Finding yourself" sounds hokey and corny, too goofy to raise; however, a major, if not THE major harvest of travel. It's the unspoken growth that holds in the forefront of your own consciousness forever, shared by no one, content to please its landlord. Only others who also have had the fortune of discovering this personal peace can share the silent calm, providing a cease-fire to arguments you have with yourself. You now have room for a retrospective analysis of your past, particularly growing up, and scrutinize from your own adults point of view. Those who were a positive influence are finally given the credit they deserve, and you can thank them silently for steering your ship so well. And you

4

select these people for continuing relationships. Those who led you down the garden path with unwise direction also come clear. Your ship can now right itself by shedding their anchor.

The mantra from the engine or the hum from bus tires on a highway is a form of hypnosis - or hypnosis itself, whatever hypnosis is. Everyone experiences deep daydreams of long rides on the highway, but the distractions of everyday life interrupt your sessions. Jumping straight back into one's obligations shortchanges the therapy. À la carte travel places no restrictions on duty; the sole responsibility lies in keeping yourself satisfied. Your time is yours, and yours alone. If a therapy session is interrupted, the diversion won't be serious enough to detain you for long. You can then go back and put the finishing touches on decisions, personal policies, etc. Or, ample time for another sitting will soon arise.

Staring into the night's mysterious, black ink was the easel where I pictured the people and scenarios with whom the conversations took place. It's an enormous healing to find the answers to the mysteries of our lives, mysteries each of us carry, be they regrets, triumphs, closet skeletons, borne crosses, dreams, wishes, hopes, questions, you name it.

KNIGHTS IN FEATHERED ARMOR RISK THE CONSUMMATE WAGER
Filipino Chickens Are Anything But Chicken

The captain nestled *The Viva Soccoro* up to the pier with a mother's gentleness. The initial impression from the boat suggested Coron, in the Calamian Group of islands in the western part of the Philippine archipelago, was nothing that adorned oil paintings. A stretch of colorless wooden houses with thatched roofs built upon stilts was the landscape.

It was Sunday, and the Filipinos combine their two religions on the same day. Staunchly Roman Catholic, they attend mass in the morning and then prepare for the afternoon service - cock fights.

This town's edifice du combat was an unpainted roof with no walls, only supports made of planks. A five-level grandstand of unpainted timbers, with seating for about 300, surrounded the ring, a steel tubing cage the height of a backyard fence and approximately ten paces square. The surface, a parched clay like the French Open's Roland Garros, kicked up no dust.

The only women were selling San Miguel beers, Cokes, chips, and a few candies from a canteen. Also in attendance was the couple who arrived with the guest of honor, the lechon.

A lechon is another sacrifice of battle - a whole roasted pig. A bamboo pole is slid unceremoniously from north to south through the gutted pig and wired down; then, poised over smoldering coals, is slowly hand-rotisseried for three to four hours resulting in a succulent, dripping, barbecued hog, and a routine ingredient of the weekly festivities.

The swinemaster hacks off chunks with a machete, grease and juices flying (in the movie Apocalypse Now, the bovine sacrifice scene near the end was a bona fide ceremony from a tribe in the Philippines). I dove into a half kilo, and with no room for manners, I did my best to eat the meat only, but with all that fat, it soon proved to be a lost cause.

I was rehearsing an apology to my cardiologist when the preliminaries began on the first bout. The two owners and their roosters entered the ring, along with the official referee and a trail of other guys with no just cause to be there except that this is the

Does Your Meter Work?!

Philippines. The ref, barking out his orders, spotted my foreign face foraging for flesh and asked if I would like to bet. I refused, as low key as possible, but became the brunt of some good-natured jokes. Within the Philippines, there is always a sentiment of welcome.

The roosters are beautiful birds. Some are snow white throughout. Others have black tails and wings with a cream chest, complete with matching head feathers cascading over their shoulders and backs like a lion's mane. Others are brilliantly colored with teals, greens, harvest golds, burnt oranges, burgundies, and liver reds.

The owners raise them from chicks, feeding special food and vitamins for strength and health. After 15 to 18 months, the gladiators are ready. On the big day, each scrapper is outfitted with a razor-sharp, curved saber about the length of a man's first finger - tied with fishing line using artistic science - pointing straight back from their right ankle. Fiercely hateful of their opponents, instinct incites them to fly up and attack with their feet. The winner, quite obviously, is the rooster that remains alive.

To prime them for the fight, each cock is held by the tail and permitted to approach. Their feet dig into the ground or run in the air in a desperate attempt to storm their foe. The owners then cradle their birds and each cock takes a few pecks at their opponent. One holds his bird's head stationary, while the other is allowed a few stabs. Then the opposing bird returns the favor.

During the warm-up, a series of hand gestures determines wagers. Holding fingers straight up indicates denominations of 10's, holding fingers sideways is for 100's, and pointing the corresponding amount straight down is for 1000's of pesos, of which there is no shortage. A bet of 1,350 pesos requires three movements. In the first, one finger points straight down, signifying "one thousand." Immediately three fingers extend horizontally, to signify "three hundred." Finally, all five digits point up, for five times ten, or fifty. A wave of the hand to the left or right indicates which bird the bettor wants. Odds are set using another round of finger semaphore that requires a Filipino gene to understand.

With the ref signaling the close of betting, and the fowls foul, sheathes are removed from the leg-knives with the utmost care (two men are needed: one holds the bird still and the other delicately slides off the protective encasement), beaks touch (like boxers touch gloves), each man takes a step back, and drops his bird to the ground.

They hunch down, neck feathers flaring out like umbrellas, their feet stepping cross-overs. One springs up; the other reflexively mirrors the move. Crashing foot long into each other, feathers fly. Dazed and confused, they both hit the ground in a tangled mess. Without stepping back, they go at it again. Except during the melee of an assault, loathsome steely-eyed stares never yield.

Approval ratings by the 35 or so watchers are high, expressed by shrieks, yells, and that distinctly Filipino effusive, thigh -slapping laughter.

One owner, about 20, is clearly nervous. In his youthful exuberance he would like nothing better than to knock off the much older man in what must be an old boys' game in a macho world.

The older man's bird is bleeding and cannot walk. Its knife-bearing leg has been slashed. The bird is unable to kick. The aggressor flies up and lands on his opponent, thrusting pecks once, twice, three times, then backs off and circles, confused. His foe is unable to move, protect himself, or fight. The referee picks up each battler by its back; each pecks once and they are dropped facing each other. The injured one tumbles on his side. The ref continues trying to revive the fight, sometimes eliciting a brief flurry, but the ten-minute maximum expires with neither combatant expiring. Muffled sighs and grumbles indicate a draw with all bets off. Both birds are wounded and exhausted and have lost any will for combat.

Bouts carry on into the evening. Few survive ten minutes to result in ties. Most matches finish in under a minute - many in a matter of seconds; a fatal stab registers somewhere in that fracas of feathers. Between matches, in a real-life Far Side cartoon, life imitates art when a fight breaks out between two owners. Money exchanges either hand to hand or by an intriguing method of folding up the bills into a small ball with two wings and thrown to helicopter across the ring. In big-city arenas, slit tennis balls stuffed with bills are chucked to winners. No loser welches on his bet. Refusing to pay or trying to run out would put the debtor in the same pot as his wrongly bet upon chicken. Returning to my hotel, I

Does Your Meter Work?!

had a plate of pancit canton - fried noodles mixed with a collection of vegetables and beef. I wasn't in the mood for chicken.

A TROPICAL WATERCOLOR
Come On In, The Water's Psychedelic

Self Contained Underwater Breathing Apparatus. By the time you say it, you're drowned. Scuba's better. I don't know if a five minute lesson, then 20 meters below sea level is a wise thing to do, but one of the advantages of diving in countries who need your money more than they need your admiration is the chance to say, "I dived and gone to heaven." El Nido, a sleepy village near the northern tip of Palawan, the most westerly island in the Philippine archipelago, is about snorkeling and diving.

The clear morning blue sky dovetailed into the deep azure of the ocean. Fifteen minutes later, at a gleaming cream-colored beach, backdropped by a sheer-faced limestone cliff, dive-master Romy strapped on my vest and tank; then he checked the breathing apparatus as I adjusted the mask, fins, and lead-weight belt (some women readers may mistake this for their husband). Squatting in chest-deep water, the first frogman lesson was to spit out the mouthpiece, take off the mask, then put everything back - all under water. To clear water from the mask, push the top of the mask against your forehead, look up, and exhale nasally. The mask fills with air and propels the water out. No problem. To clear water and saliva from your mouth, push a button on the mouthpiece. Forced air runs through and out two exhaust ports. Piece of cake. When descending, pressure builds in the ears as in an airplane, but worse. Plug your nose and blow out nasally. The pressure detours to your ears, which go boing! boing! in stereo. No sweat. To defog the mask on the inside, delicately break the seal around the mask and let a trickle of water in. Look down, swish the water over the glass, look up, clear the mask. Voila! A clear view on the situation. Take a peek at the depth meter.

I'M 20 METERS DOWN!!!!

A couple of deep, steady breaths calmed my panic and it was time to enjoy the voyage - 20,000 millimeters under the sea.

The underwater world is indeed a sight to behold, an enchanted kingdom we've come to tour, thumbing our noses at Mother Nature by becoming amphibian, infiltrating into an environment she hadn't intended humans to occupy. Ol' Mom has done some of her finest work down here. The kaleidoscope of ethereal colors is too perfect to be reproduced. The brilliant hues

10

and superb trimmings make magic occur. A giant tortoise, its shell an axe handle wide, hovered not far away. One graceful swish of its paddles put it around and behind. I turned to see another equally polished swish, and then it vanished.

A wrap of unexploded dynamite, which Romy picked up to examine, rested on the ocean floor. Fishermen use it as a cheap substitute for a net. It had to be inert; Romy wouldn't have been fooling with it otherwise, I nervously reasoned.

The view was hypnotic and, at times, for a split second, I instinctively wanted to spit out an encumbrance in my mouth, but reality quickly bit where a deep breath and mouthpiece clearing provided solace. The underwater silence was deafening, interrupted only by the bubbles of exhaling. At the surface, the sun broke into a 1000 laser lights zipping past and ending on the ocean floor. Looking skyward, I strained to see angels appear; a shot of salty brine corroded into my nasal cavity. Clear the mask.

Each ten meters of depth is equivalent to one atmosphere, a unit of pressure equal to the pressure of air at sea level. Each meter of descent increases the consumption of air and, because of my amateurness, 20 meters was the maximum safe zone from the surface. The greatest danger is losing air. The buddy system of sharing the mouthpiece of another's functioning system on the way up is the emergency procedure. If the body ascends faster than bubbles rise, nitrogen builds more rapidly than it can naturally dissipate through the skin, causing the bends. A number of physiological problems threaten a diver with a nitrogen bubble in their bloodstream. Therefore, rising slowly is imperative; not having to go far to the surface reduces risk.

There was Romy looking for me. Our eyes did the smiling, our mouths crowded with apparatus. He waved, "Follow me" and with a silky smooth frog-kick, left me in his wake. I tried to mirror his maneuver but got so leg-tied, I think I went backwards. He turned to see me losing ground and serenely waited while I paddled up. The colors went on and on. A mobile random rainbow, an exploded Partridge Family bus, magic mushrooms were never this good.

The tank inflates the vest at the push of a button; another releases the air to give that sinking feeling. Throughout the dive, air slowly leaks into the vest. Releasing this latent air is another of the tasks. Unfortunately, nogoodnik swirling ocean currents slowly, continually spiraled us to the surface, terminating the dive prematurely. I was fooled, constantly releasing the vest's air, trying to sink without success.

Like a depth-charged U-boat survivor, I bobbed among the swells. The weight of the tank kept me face up. Floating on my back, I stretched mouth muscles that were sore from the unfamiliar workout of managing the life-preserving mouthpiece. SPLOOSH. HACK. COUGH. The salty sea burned my eyes and sinus tissues, a punishment for all the facial contortions too ugly for public view. I constantly inflated the vest to remain buoyant. Tapped out, I spotted a close-by resting point. Eternity had eroded the limestone cliff, forming a shelf 18 inches above sea level. I held onto this edge while the boat trolled over with Romy in tow, ending the dive.

GETTING AROUND THE LAST FRONTIER OF THE PHILIPPINES CAN BE TRICKY

The Philippines unites some 7,000 islands. Palawan, the most westerly island of the archipelago is a local name meaning *Gate of Combat*. The island was a barrier against the violence of invaders past that emerged from the South China Sea. Nationally, it's nicknamed *The Last Frontier of the Philippines*.

In the far north of Palawan sits the sleepy town of El Nido, or "nest" in Spanish. After a few days of scuba diving and auditioning for the lead role as a sloth, I leafed through the guidebook to decide my next move. A boat to the city of Zamboanga on the island of Mindanao, the southernmost island of the Philippines, then a ferry to Sabah in East Malaysia on the island of Borneo ripened into a funky idea. The next question: could it be done? Apparently, such a service existed at one point, but civil strife and the hassles of international borders forced its closure. Then Kenny from Sweden recounted how he had crossed a few weeks earlier from Sabah to Zamboanga.

My spirits lifted. But to accomplish the feat required a pump boat back to an ugly little town, Taytay, then a jeepney or bus to Puerto Princessa to prospect out the next leg. During my time in El Nido, I'd heard horror stories of excursions from Puerto Princessa to Taytay because of Palawan's iffy transportation and lack of hard-surfaced roads. Similar versions of winching, pushing, and pulling buses, jeepneys, trucks etc., while the pushers were up to their ears in mud, took anywhere from nine to 21 hours, depending on the inevitable rain.

I packed up the next morning, and after a relatively quick 2 1/2 hour jaunt on the boat, made it to Taytay. The scenery was ravishing. Walls of mangrove defended foliated shorelines. Teal-blue water licked at uninhabited gleaming, creamy beaches backdropped by vertically faced limestone cliffs hundreds of feet straight up. Craggy, weathered, and arranged in rows, the cliffs resembled regal slices of bread forming a stony karst loaf.

Providentially, a jeepney was just pulling away for Puerto Princessa (Spanish for Port Princess). Hopping on now was a much better alternative to spending the evening unearthing dubious information for the next day's transport, then sleeping the night in the town's bunker of a hotel.

To augment the adventure, two hard-assed looking guys in camouflage dress, M-16's equipped with grenade launchers, and lots of ammo climbed on as an escort. I pulled out my camera, took a picture, and then said, "OOPS." Rough-looking dude passengers began offering cigarettes and candies with inappropriate friendliness, all the while glancing at my tightly clutched bag. I knew my stuff was the object of their conversation, their phony nonchalance betrayed by truth-telling body language.

With Palawan a long way from home and the rule of law, I could have been easy pickings for anyone. Should the two palookas with the hardware be in cahoots or feeling underpaid, they would have loved to uncover the $11,000, albeit in traveler's checks, $1000 camera, credit card, and Canadian passport I was packing.

The seating, designed to keep capital costs low and for the more delicately framed indigenes, pulverized my buns -- and the back of my head from smacking the low roof -- over dirt roads which ranged from merely uneven to downright jarring.

A bump skipped a bag out and down the road. I scanned around. Everyone was in his private dream world. I hurriedly tapped my neighbor's shoulder to point out the problem and he delivered a scream that put seven geckoes out of business. Brakes locked and faces jolted awake. The jeepney's gears clunked; the transmission whined in reverse; someone jumped down to retrieve the sack; then asked to whom it belonged. The bag's proprietor, the ringleader of my group of bandits, had been quasi-asleep, his head bouncing around on a neck made of rubber. With his indifferent hiss and nary a nod of appreciation, only cryptic stares of hostility, we continued. The back was abuzz for ten minutes or so as the load of passengers dissected how the lone white wolf had spoken up and rescued the wayward luggage.

A rather steep hill presented itself. The tranny cleared its throat going up into third gear as the driver gunned the engine to take a run. Back into fourth. Mud blazed behind the spinning dual rear wheels. Whomp! Big puddle. Water everywhere. Chickens squawking. Bigger headache. The speed quickly dropped from 25 mph to less than ten.

Scrunch ... back into third.

Eight mph; six; four; three; two; barely one. Mud everywhere.

Don't gear down again.

Crawling, clawing, begging. The crest approached. Two mph, then three.

SKLANK! Second gear.

Five, eight.

Skwitch. Third gear again.

The rooster-tail of muck tapered off, liberating gales of Filipino laughter and chatter. The driver turned to eye his bevy. Biggest smile of them all.

Fourth gear 'cause who's yer Daddy?

With only a few tough spots and no unscheduled stops, we arrived at Puerto Princessa in a record-breaking less than eight hours. Relief flooded my capillaries when my buddies loaded up their chickens and bags just outside of Puerto Princessa and withdrew as a group. Lost Luggage Leader, a rooster in tow, plugged one of his nostrils. HORK. Out came a day's worth of booger. Then the other for balance.

All in all, a propitious day's travel, considering the warning yarns I had heard reported by others: the day had begun way back in El Nido, it was still early evening in Puerto Princessa. And I still had all my things. A wonderful day traveling in the farthest corner of the Philippines

<u>YOU CAN'T GET HIGHER IN SOUTH-EAST ASIA</u>

At the edge of where I stood, the plummeting canyon dropped straight down ... a long way. The wind blew in gusts. Wonky legs sent a weak but distinct message to retreat from the brink. Dawn's early light began to awaken, turning high clouds into swaths of burnt orange and flaming red. Ever so slowly, the sun clawed its way up and around a distant jagged, rocky apex, and shone white light against far away jutting curves. Gargantuan slabs of rock formed a massive patio, arcing gracefully away, its edge diving down to the far below cloud-cover that shrouded the jungle-covered foothills of the Mother mountain. Persistently, the shadow's line approached until, finally, the rays of warmth attacked my shivering. Gripping the camera tightly, my poorly functioning fingers pressed hard on the shutter release to record the spectacular scene.

The best-known expedition in Sabah, one of two states in East Malaysia on the island of Borneo, is to climb the highest peak in South-East Asia - Mount Kinabalu at 13,451 feet. Mount Kinabalu is the spiritual home of Dusan, and its name derives from AKINABALU, revered place of the dead. Standing on that lip, personal extinction was only half a step away.

Thirty-six hours earlier, the air at the park entrance – at 5000 feet - was refreshingly cool compared to the lower altitude tropical heat of Malaysia, and the dense jungle was absolutely green, green, green. Spirits were high and wits competed among us travelers who had ad-libbed into groups of eight to share the guide costs. We were unsure what to expect. The only first-hand report had come from a veteran of the odyssey who was back down the same afternoon as our arrival. Lying in his bed of our six-bed dorm, he chuckled and giggled, saying only, "It's hard ... but worth it." What does that mean? How hard is hard? Whaddaya mean "worth it?" To whom? How?

At 7:30 the next morning, a bus lugged up a paved road to mile 0 at 6200 feet. The trail began easily, over a boardwalk and past a scintillating waterfall. From there on, with nature as the winning-bid architect, rarely was the track a flat path on an incline as had been the speculation. Each step climbed a stair, each stair made of rock, carved-out stones, tree roots, or a few man-made ladders. No two stairs climbed the same height, some many little steps melted together, others required ropes and a helping hand from the climber in front. If no help was forthcoming, grab anything, a branch, a small tree, the next step, another root; claw the dirt. At times, I used the strap from my bag as a pull rope, snagging something and pulling myself up. Add to the potion a combination of trail, dry creek beds, wet creek beds, sheer-faced stone, cliffs, gravel, planks, ropes, rocks, boulders, sand, mud holes, water holes, rest points, flowers, jungle, squirrels, rats, birds, waterfalls, clouds, wind, mist, rain, downpours, and sunshine all in one direction - UP. A vertical witch's brew.

Finally, thankfully, at approximately 5 p.m., the first huts for the partial nights stay appeared, mile 9.6 at 11,000 feet. Our group collected in the canteen for a "What did we get ourselves into?" therapy session. We'd only just begun when the rain exploded with a mighty crash. A mini-Niagara formed on the next cliff over and thundered past the window, but because of its astonishing power, it seemed only a few steps away. Then, in a chillingly choreographed supernatural display, Mother Nature slammed shut her valves. The near vertical river vanished and the clouds deserted to provide a glimpse for the next day. In a blink, the clouds gray veil recloaked the rock and the water again pounded past.

A lousy, frosty sleep ended at plus or minus 2:30; the protocol was to reach the summit for sunrise. A nearly full moon dominated the starry sky. The climb's final 2.5 to 3 miles, above the tree line, comprised flat, steep, colossal sheets of rock.

Finally, the final peak point, mile 14.1 at 13,451 feet. The temperature was 35°, the wind about 25 mph. I had on a t-shirt, cotton pants, acrylic sweater, plastic poncho, socks, and sandals. Other travelers garbed similar attire. Who knew what it was all about? My hands were swollen and frozen; feet soaked and more frozen; lips stinging, chapped, and bleeding. The hardy souls who needed to reach the peak waved. I still needed another 400 or so yards. Were we having a good time? Nyet. I took another jittery picture instead.

With the photo shoot completed, one last point remained: who goes up must come down. The final leg began as a group, but Anders from Sweden - early twenties, fit as a fiddle, and in rut - and two of his contemporaries, a German doctor, and another European stud, ran down to cap their challenge. I suspected a certain national pride at stake for the first to the bottom. Our guide didn't care, his job finished at the top; he was at home and immune from international competitions.

Anikka, Kristina, (Ander's traveling companions) and I ambled down slowly. Too spent, we had no choice. If it's true misery enjoys company, then we were the Three Stooges. Jokes and self-ridicule united our misery. Howling with laughter (it was the opposite of crying) at our ineptness, each 1/3 mile trail mark took longer and longer to reach.

Female porters ferried supplies up to the canteen. Fifty-pound bottles of propane, hung by a loop over their foreheads with a pad protecting their skin from the rope, rested on their backs.

We laughed and limped our way to the bottom, last off the hill. A young, attractive damsel in distress convinced a valiant stalwart to carry her down the final remaining way and they nipped us at the finish line.

We pulled ourselves aboard a waiting bus (hallucinations read "hearse") and slunk into the seats like Rocky after round 15 (there ain't gonna be no rematch). At the park entrance, Anders roosted on a stone wall, looking fresh as a farm egg, and snickered:

"My goodness, you Canadians are, how do you say, wimps?"

Wimp would cover it.

After 12 dead-to-the-world hours of sleep and a pleasant breakfast, we stood on the opposite sides of the highway, thumbing to our next destinations: east to Sandakan for my comrades and west to Kota Kinabalu for me.

"Hey, here comes a truck! Get your thumbs out. They love Swedes in this country. Sorry, no brake lights. Losers!"

"No one's lining up to take you! And there's only one of you. You're three times the loser!"

After 10 minutes, a truck, loaded with pipe and then them, disappeared around the corner. My ride coincided with their departure where I was dropped off in front of my hostel in Kota Kinabalu. First thing, I took a nap. As I dropped off, I recalled the mandatory insurance policies. The apparent money grab now made sense. Health insurance valued at $5000 was enough to get the patient down. And for those too broken to recover, the $5000 life insurance policy was enough extra to send the occasional abruptly denationalized body home.

NIAH CAVE
<u>Not Just Any Hole in the Wall</u>

Flying flashes of movement whisk near the cave's ceiling. A distant shine from the other end becomes something to journey towards. The jutting edges and contours of the floor weaken the light's zipping rays. Craggy edges hold stalactites fast to the ceiling. The air cools and becomes dank, clammy. A thin slime coats the planked handrails and wooden stairways that snake through the vastness, the little light from the entrance slowly dwindling as I make my way further inside Niah Cave, one of the world's largest caves located in the state of Sarawak in East Malaysia on the island of Borneo. The atmosphere warms, the lumber is less slick, until the plankway ends just short of exiting the other side. The cave itself, a gigantic tunnel, houses another smaller cave. The Painted Cave's walls exhibit drawings dating back 1,000 years, their origins still veiled in mystery and debate.

Millions of sleeping bats inhabit the cave by day. By night, with the bats out playing, a like number of swifts dwell in their nests, of which the Chinese harvest to make their famous bird's nest soup. The cave floor, thick with guano - the combined faeces of the cave's occupants - is carted away and sold for fertilizer. Armed guards protect these gathering areas.

An hour plankwalk through the jungle to the cave's entrance and back is alive with plants and trees and Fauvist butterflies and lizards and flowers and streams and water snakes and squirrels and crickets and frogs and birds and mosses. Everything is green. The jungle's canopy blocks the sun; even the shade casts a greenish hue. A cluster of trees staves off a brief shower. Hang a left onto the narrow, derelict planks halfway to the cave, and you end up at a village of typical Malaysian longhouses rising in a marshy clearing.

Don't be thrown by The Wild Man From Borneo myth. Malaysia, in spite of occasional bad press, is one of the most stable, peaceful, enjoyable, prosperous countries in Asia. Besides, the lights go out early in this Muslim country.

Two miles from Batu Niah (the town of Niah, you can walk or take a sliver of a boat for 10 ringgit), Malaysia Parks has constructed magnificent cabins available as private or dorm rooms.

Does Your Meter Work?!

They come complete with thick mattresses, full pillows, varnished hardwood walls and floors, desks, night tables, clothes cupboards, ceramic-tiled bathrooms, fluorescent lights, five-speed adjustable ceiling fans, hot-water showers, bath mats, sinks to wash clothes, a huge common area filled with teak and hardwood furniture plushly upholstered, and so on. The tailored grounds are cut tight, and surrounding verandas provide a cushy sunshade. The entire site seeks an answer to, "What is this jewel doing *here*?"

Nightly concerts include singing birds duetting with croaking frogs, and harmonized with the background sounds of the crickets. In the distance, other birds cackle and chirp to round out the orchestra. Each night rainstorms with the accompanying lightning exposition. Like lapping waves, it's a soothing barbiturate.

You can rent a bed in a four-bed dorm for 10 ringgit ($1=3.8MYR), or take the whole room for 40. Class 3 chalets for four cost 120 while Class 2 chalets go for 180. If you only play the big rooms, the VIP Resthouse price tags sit at 200 and 250. Or, you can tent it for four ringgit per campsite. You'll be charged a Photography Permit Fee: five ringgit for a still camera, ten for a video camera, and 200 for professional filming.

The only toad in the punchbowl is the food. A restaurant is available, but it's appropriately called a canteen, serving basic kebabs, nasi goreng, and roti.

Go to www.sarawaktourism.com and click on Niah Caves.

DIGITAL TRANSPORTATION
A Simple Bet Turns Into A Wild Ride Across Borneo

"Uh, no Carl, I'm gonna hitch."

Backpacking alone on the cheap allows the freedom to blurt things before your brain can stop it. After months of criss-crossing Asia on everything from boats to goats, I found myself at Niah Caves National Park - one of Earth's largest cave systems - on the island of Borneo. Millions of bats reside there during the day and an equal number of swallows at night, give or take a few hundred thousand. A snazzy hostel tucks into the rainforest nearby.

"Go West, Young Man," wasn't a common phrase in this rustic little hideaway, except to Carl, a Dutch man staying there, and myself. Since the next day we were both heading to Kuching, the most westerly city of consequence in East Malaysia, 500-plus miles away, he suggested that we team up. A bus to Sibu, an overnight, then highspeed ferry to Kuching would shuttle us in early the next morning. Carl wasn't a lout; I just couldn't bear the thought of his voice and the hiss of public bus tires simultaneously.

"You're gonna hitchhike?" he asked.

"Uh huh, and I'll get there before you."

"You'll take a week, or die."

Could be.

Shortly after 8 a.m. the next morning, I hung an ambivalent thumb, without Carl, and within 90 seconds a car stopped and took me to the main highway, putting me 20 miles ahead of the Dutch Resistance. His bus wouldn't depart for another hour. My driver drove left, I walked right, and the first car took me about 12 miles. I waited ten minutes or so for an eventual 30-mile ride. After ten minutes, my rested thumb pulled out a plum. Two lovely Malay women, late twenties, were headed to Bintulu, which was the end of my arbitrary first leg and point of departure for the second, the trip to Sibu.

"What was I doing begging rides on the highway?" they wanted to know.

Westerners were not poor Malays, or conservative Muslims, and their fates might hang heavily on the minds of

Does Your Meter Work?!

Malays. When I explained about the race, they giggled, and we settled back as friends on a journey where decorum gave way for speed. About five miles from Bintulu, we slowed suddenly before a highway sign that said, "SIBU, NEXT LEFT." Throughout the lift, their friendliness had me dreaming of Malaysian hugs and kisses under palm trees, but reality dropped a coconut onto my coconut. Doing a maybe and hitting a dead end was an unwanted alternative to fantasy cuddling, so I confessed the desire for my Kuching rather than their Bintulu and unloaded. The race was getting pricey.

The highway at the crossroad was busy but unripe for rides. After a long 20 minutes of standing between the road and a quarry, and after I had been punished for my fantasies by being pelted with sand, someone stopped for a mere two miles. Another 20 minutes of burnt-up daylight, and I netted a 30 mile lift, just as I wavered between racing and just plain arriving.

The traffic was so thin, and a light rain had started to fall. I was fishing for my poncho when a car coming from the wrong way suddenly slowed, U-turned on the highway, the window rolled down, and a smiley face invited me aboard. Why was he stopping and turning from the opposite direction? In the car, the man explained that he had passed by a few minutes earlier, then had an attack of conscience and couldn't leave me outside in the rain. He was a Malaysian-Chinese businessman in the logging industry, educated in England, spoke excellent English, was very bright, and headed to Sibu. We shared our experiences with travel abroad and with crowds of lovely lady drivers, and we asked and answered each other's questions during terrific conversations. He was so interesting, the race had become a non-starter. In fact, I never mentioned it. He adamantly insisted on paying for lunch, a toothsome bowl of noodle soup, claiming "Malaysian hospitality."

In Sibu he dropped me at a ferry. On the boat, a Chinese couple candidly told me the idea of hitching was nuts, and that racing was, well, not too swift -- but what the heck, they said, come on with us. An hour later, on the highway again, and using my ever-lengthening shadow as a sundial, the sun set slowly and my reservations rose. I needed a long-haul transport truck. No sooner did this thought insert and extract when two young fellows running empty from Sibu to Kuching rumbled up. They cleared the rear sleeping area, offered whatever they had from cigarettes to mineral water, referred to me as "sir," and drove that lorry like they'd stolen it.

An hour and a half out of Kuching, the sky pitch black, the front tire blew. My guys, cursing in Malay, kicked the spare out of its hiding spot. Flat. Use one of the dual rear tires - the nuts were too tight, rusted on. Call the office on the cellular - no answer.

We had broken down in front of an army base: half the National Guard stood around looking for a solution and puzzling who the hell the white guy was. I queried, while slapping mosquitoes, whether the military wouldn't have the tools to do the job.

"Of course, but that would be government property and off limits for Malay citizens."

My chauffeurs were totally race-minded, and to my complete surprise they decided to flag down a bus for their competition-minded friend. They would sleep in their truck until help could come the next morning.

The nights get inky black at the equator, and even with a 3/4 moon, it was still too dark for bus drivers to see our waving in time. The army boys weren't missing out on this; they came to life and launched a roadblock. Five or six attempts to secure a Kuching-bound vehicle begot no success and a lot of laughing, splattered soldiers. Finally, a family of Chinese Malaysians riding in an SUV agreed to an extra passenger. I thanked the revived military, blessed the Chinese, and embraced my helmsmen, offering to buy the latter a beer of gratitude the next day if we could get together. This race was getting costly. My merry companions had a simple caveat for their entertainer: "Oh no, no! If our office sees us with you, we're fired!"

Beginning at the outskirts of Kuching, my latest driver initiated high-level discussions about suitable accommodations. Generally, most Asians expect that any tourist wants snazzy digs on holiday. I was difficult. Their picture of the white race had no room for hitchhiking Canadians with thin wallets, but I finally managed to convince my new friends to think cheap. They dropped the name of one establishment, a name that I recognized as the first choice suggested in the Fat-Cat's guide book. Standing on the sidewalk outside choice number one, in full diplomatic mode, I thanked them for their assistance and advice, and waved with real gratitude as they roared away.

The hotel was expensive but, thank Wall Street, it was also full. I went to another across the street - still too much. Went to another - locked up tighter than a bank vault. Went to another - no vacancy at any price. Then I remembered that I was in Asia, where the expensive is offered to the visitor before the cheap is even remembered. Returned to the expensive hostelry; they magically produced the heretofore nonexistent cheaper room, and I was in Kuching for real. Suddenly, I remembered the race, and wistfully, for win or lose, it was over.

Past 11 by now, my eyes felt tired, itchy from sand and wind, and the lids were heavy; I skimmed an old newspaper I found in my lair, and turned off the light. Laying in the dark, I imagined Carl still in Sibu setting his alarm to catch his morning high-speed ferry. I fell asleep realizing that in a whirling storm of sand and rain, Chinese and Malays, teamsters and troopers, strange men and fascinating women, my race had been won. I closed my weary eyes and slept the sleep of the surprised, contented, and freshly informed.

THUMB MORE

You just read a story with a hitch, a wild day hitchhiking across Borneo to Kuching, the most westerly city on the island. Hitching is like heroin, they're both addicting, and I was jonesing for more.

I flew across the Johor Strait to Johor Bahru, the Western Malaysian city across the causeway from Singapore, then walked away from the airport and hung a thumb. In no time, a Curious George in a pick-up stopped and took me the couple of miles to a highway junction.

"Why you no take a bus?" he wanted to know. "I give you money."

I said no thanks, he went left, shaking his head, and I right, heading north for Mersing on the east coast. Today's highway snacks were an orange, raisins, and butter coconut cookies to give the always-present bottle of water something to wash down.

Hitching proved difficult, taking me nearly an hour to scarf up a ride on a double-laned highway filthy with cars. No one ever actually stopped; my eventual ride was a man returning to his vehicle parked near where I stood. He explained that everyone was leery about slowing and stopping on the superhighway. So why was he less leery than the rest?

He took me a little off course, but on this hot, humid day a ride was a ride and he went basically north. Fifty or so miles later in a sleepy town, he pointed my next direction, shook his head, and was outta there. Another hour later my shoulder tired, thumb drooped and depressed, a nice man, a teacher by trade, in a clunker was going the distance to Mersing. He gave a guided tour as we rode past plantations of bananas, tea, durian, palm oil, rice, and rubber. From a distance, the rows looked like any old flora anywhere on Earth, but knowing what these green bits would turn into appealed to my imaginative side.

The rainy season had taken over the east coast of Malaysia, and a sprinkle that started at the edge of this small town turned into a full-blown storm by the time we hit the center. Professor Plant kindly dropped me at a hostel.

A nice, decent young guy from the Czech Republic lodged in the dorm. He had scraped enough together to get to Australia to sweat it out washing dishes to earn more money for English lessons. After a year, satisfied with his new improved language abilities, he economized another year with the goal of traveling South-East Asia before returning home. Absolutely on top of the world, pride pouring from his pores in an unpretentious humility, he described his adventure. We talked for an hour or so, his Czech-English dictionary and notepad nestled in his lap.

Don't forget the Australian father and son combo. Dad boasted two primary talents -- first, raucous farting while parading around in his underwear, and second, failing to flush the toilet. His chip-off-the-old-block didn't know if Christmas this year fell on December 25th or 26th. It's a good thing they're family...it would be a shame to waste two houses on them.

The next morning I packed up early, left the raisins behind because something chewed up the box overnight, and stood on the highway under gray, dry clouds. Again, rides weren't growing on trees. Half an hour later two blokes took me about 10 miles. Another half hour wait then 50 more miles. No sooner were we under way when the rain detonated and never let up until it was time to get rid of me.

As I exited the car, I scrambled open my poncho and struggled to keep my two bags under its protective cloak. With only my nose and left thumb protruding from beneath the teal polyethylene, I tried to appear as pathetic as possible, hoping to strike guilt into someone.

A bus sped up. In the lower right-hand corner of the windshield was a sign. Squinting through the rain to catch a glimpse of the tiny letters, nearly even with my position, the words became clear. TERRENGANU! MY NEXT DESTINATION!

"STOP, STOP!" my waving hands cried, far too late. The bus splashed by. Who wants to stop and pick up a drowned rat? A car pulled up. The window opened a crack. A Chinese man and his young son smiled through the slit.

"Where are you going?" asked Dad.

"Terrenganu," I squeaked, with a glimmer of hope.

"Oh, no, sorry," he said.

Where are *you* going," I countered, precipitation running down my face.

"I'm going there," he announced, pointing across the street smiling, "for breakfast."

Another bus. Where's it going? Look hard, here it comes, eyes...don't fail me now, a little closer...TERRANGANU AGAIN! STOP, STOP! SPLOOSH!!!!!!!!

Forget it.

Soon after, three men who couldn't speak English assumed I wanted a bus and took me a short distance, maybe 10 miles, to a bus station. I slogged onto some public transportation bound for Terranganu where I commandeered the next bus to Kota Bahru, near the Thai border, and the left turn for the East-West Highway across to Penang.

The next day gifted blue skies, sunshine, and a brightened mood. Two rides backtracked me a half an hour south in order to turn west. An old Toyota hatchback pulled up. A spike-haired cool dude with shades on his face, another pair hanging from his T-shirt, another dangling from the rear-view mirror, and three more scattered on the dash was my first westbound lift. Fun fur covered the interior, and a ring of turkey balls did a full lap around the ceiling. He smiled (no English), I smiled, he cranked the tunes to about 9.5, and when the heads of the cassette player weren't dragging too badly, we rocked to The Scorpions blasting out of vibrating speakers, 25 miles down the highway.

At a national park, a fifteen-minute walk through the jungle then across a snazzy suspension bridge reached a 17-foot waterfall. The equatorial sun added to my creepy-dirty feeling from a lousy sleep and two days of no *planned* shower. I crawled down a short, steep bank, tied my bag and clothes in a tree, crab-walked over the polished, glassy rock, and eased into the fall. The water spilled over and massaged my weary muscles, pounding into my shoulders, neck, and back. I moved back from the tiring force, behind the rush, and leaned against the rock wall. Then, moderately recovered, I drifted back into the water's potency, finding the spot where the mass times acceleration was just the right balance of power and soothing.

On the divided four-lane superhighway that stretches north to south from Thailand to Singapore, only a few cars rocketed by until a giggly old man of Indian descent seated in a rust-bucket Toyota pickup stopped. He drove the cross-country eight hours

Does Your Meter Work?!

twice a week, buying fish in Singapore and selling them in a Thai market. Friendly and helpful, and nodding favorably because someone was goofy enough to hitch in Malaysia, he dropped me near the beginning of the causeway that connects the mainland to the island of Penang and its big city, Georgetown, or G'town. A total of nine rides from nodders and shakers, rock stars and rock heads skipped my carcass across the East-West Highway, covering the 250 or so miles. I finally surrendered to a bus after the third driver shook his head saying, "uh, uh" to alabaster guys with their ashen digits hanging out on the road.

SWEPT AWAY ON A PARASAIL

Parasailing. Isn't the whole point of parachuting to go down? The suit seemed awfully earth-centered, anyway. A girdle fit around the torso and two straps slid under my arms and wrapped over top of the shoulders to fall in front, then another two straps came from behind and up between my legs. Everything clamped together at my chest, then cinched tight à la Hannibal Lecter. A parachute hooked to the harness's shoulder points then a long, double pronged rope grappled to the same clamps. The other end of the rope attached to a boat just off shore. Sixty or so feet of the rope sat coiled on the sand.

"Ready?" the ground crew quizzed.

"I think..."

"GOOOO!!!!" they screamed to the driver.

The boat powered its 200 hp motor. Like a fuse on a bomb that Wile E. Coyote's set for Roadrunner's destruction, the pile of line dwindled before my wide-open eyes. Beep-Beep. The only instruction I ever received was to run as the line went taut. Run?! How? I had the chance for about maybe two lousy baby steps in fluffy sand, then before the chance to chicken out, straight up and gone.

The sunbathers grew smaller and smaller and the seagulls bigger and bigger. They'd seen this movie before and dispassionately banked away. Settling into the harness, my frame jerked about until I found someone's ankles patting against my chest; one of the group from the beach had come along. He had grabbed the gut-ropes, monkey-climbed up my back, and was sitting on my shoulders before I could say, "tickets, please."

With a thrilling panorama of the beach, we sped across the bay. The cool briny wind bounced against my face, the only sounds my screams of delight, or fear - I still hadn't decided. At the end of the cove, the boat turned sharply then coasted, the rope-lag wafting us down. Everything was dead calm, quiet as a cat burglar. Like the echo in a seashell, the cooler air sang in my ears. Gravity hunched my torso. My stowaway asked, "Good, good?" All I could say was, "Yeah, good," thinking about how so far, all of my things were still in the same places as they had started.

30

Does Your Meter Work?!

I had watched the different landings. My request was a touch down where the customer slowly plunges until he hits the ocean, then the admiral guns the engine, dragging the parachutist along the surface, then up again to eventually land near shore.

Instead, a bigger, whiter, bubblier wake said the propeller had burst on again, and then the sound of the engine caught up with lightspeed. The rope tightened, heaving us upwards, and heaving was suddenly on my mind as I felt the rope tethering some nasty crotch grab. My guidenurse steered us for Option B - a dry landing.

My co-pilot (I later branded him "The Monkey Man" -- he took this as the ultimate compliment) pulled and leaned inland, swinging over the beach. The boat cut power. The beach crew ran along, trying to keep up. The Monkey Man instructed me carefully in the subtleties of Earth-arrival, "Running, running". I wondered how to sell my feet on that idea because, faster than the bottom of the canyon arrives for Mr. Coyote, the hot sand approached. My soles brushed one step, two steps on the terra if somewhat shifty firma. For a second, home was welcoming me, when a gust of wind that the crew anticipated refilled the parachute, yanking us up what seemed miles but were probably only a few feet. The Monkey Man disembarked from his branch, synchronizing perfectly with a few final strategic tugs to plop us softly down.

Parasailing demands recollection in tranquility, at least for this normally grounded roadrunner. Reflected over a cool drink by the world's reddest sunset, parasailing is more thrills than one man hitchhiking across Asia deserves, but, like a date with Michelle Pfeiffer, or a dream of one, the experience appears too brief, a soreing soaring that was over too soon. Phuket, in the south of Thailand, has the perfect setting for dreams of flying like an angel.

THTILL MORE THUMBIN'

After 12 daze of soaking up the sun on Thailand's famous beach at Phuket, my Scandinavian pals were on their way home, and my idle days were growing too listless. Next stop: Bangkok. A flight gouged 3000 baht ($120). The train was full for another week or more. The bus, a red-eye special @ 550B, departed Phuket in the afternoon and arrived in Bangkok at 6 a.m. Racing against this schedule and budget by hitching sounded like the most fun. Thumbing in Malaysia had been easy but were Thais as laid back? Would they want money for lifts? Impeded by only fear and good judgment, I decided to hop a mini bus to the airport for 150B and get off on the highway.

January 1st. I met the mini-bus at 7 a.m. We snaked around to a few hotels picking up hung-over passengers and dropped them at the airport. The driver let me out on his way back to the beach. I hung a thumb and the first ride stopped in minutes. They advised the trip would be only about 20 miles, nevertheless I hopped in the back of their little truck to get some distance in.

In a mirror image, five minutes later I was again in the back of a little truck for 30 miles. The hot, black, composite finishing broiled my butt. The guy drove like a wild man, passing others with impunity, surprising them with his Caucasian cargo. I held my camera up as if to take their pictures, rousing big smiles and frantic waves.

The next car took five seconds to stop. A lovely couple, they ad-libbed an invitation to their nearby destination, a New Year's Day party. The air-conditioning was going hard and the cooling was soothing, but I'd been the main attraction in Asia before; lots of smiling, nodding and the same questions over and over. I preferred to take a crack at Bangkok, still nearly 500 miles away. I bailed out at their turn and re-acquainted myself with early afternoon tropical heat.

Another short wait of maybe two minutes and 15 more miles. After five minutes, a mini-van pulled up. I thought he was a public vehicle and misinterpreted my dangling thumb for flagging him down.

He stood at his door and, raising his chin, asked, "Go where?"

32

"Bangkok."

"Okay," he said with gentleness.

"Do you want money?"

"No."

Perfect. He threw my bags into the side door. The van carried his family heading home to Bangkok after their holiday. Inside were scattered kids, clothes, blankets, litter, and two women. I climbed over a mountain of stuff and claimed the rear seat.

This isn't a van, it's an archaeological dig.

No one spoke any English, just turned often to look and smile. At the first meal stop, I was busy with a second helping when I counted four kids. I had only tallied three previously. What else was hiding within our freight? The adults tried treating my meals and snacks, but I protested. They, in turn, refused my offers to buy a meal. At another break, a nice waterfall, holiday revelers soaped themselves down and swam in the pools. I sat about fidgeting inside, smiling outside.

Bangkok or Bust.

An abnormal number of bathroom breaks slowed the last few hours. Father drove too quickly into each rest stop, hit the brakes too hard for his passengers' comfort, and scooted to the toilet rooms. Each time, the ladies-in-waiting gestured that I also could use the facilities but it was an unspoken apology for all the stops. Poor father. There's nothing funny about the Siam Sphincter.

Phuket to Bangkok is around 600 miles. My hosts and I disconnected on a quiet, dark street somewhere in Bangkok about 2 a.m. – 15 hours after I left my Phuket hotel. A taxi for 150 baht landed me in *Freak Show Central* - Khao San Road. Phuket to Bangkok cost 300B for transport and four hours ahead of the bus. I rang and rang the bell at a guesthouse until finally granted entry, took a dorm bed, brushed my teeth, only woke one person clambering into the 8-bed room, and fell asleep.

ANGKOR WAT - A FAR, FAR BETTER PLACE THAN I HAVE EVER BEEN

The storied ancient civilization of the Khmer, centered in war-torn Cambodia, spanned approximately from 800 until 1200 AD. They rose to rule most of the region including present-day Laos, Vietnam, Thailand, and even parts of China because of a peculiar quirk of nature.

Each spring, as the run-off courses down the Mekong River from the Himalayas, the volume of water becomes too great, and backwashes into the country's largest lake, Tonle Sap (Tonle means big lake, and Sap is fresh, or not salt). For four months, the flooding quadruples the lake to more than 120 miles long and 50 miles wide, submerging trees and vegetation that nourishes a huge supply of fish and rice. As the Mediterranean flourished because of abundant food, so did the area of Tonle Sap.

Indian traders, cosmopolitan and architecturally ostentatious, were blown by the monsoons to Asia, and six months later they would blow home. As a result, early Khmers venerated Brahma, the creator god of the Hindu religion. The Indians traveled extensively in the area, hence the designation Indo-China.

A seven month siege by Mongol and Thai hordes finally led to the Khmer downfall. Eventually, the Khmers shed their Thai captors, where the Buddhist philosophy of suffering settled in with the downtrodden peasants.

Left behind is Angkor Wat, not one spot but the generic name used for a collection of fortresses, temples, and structures that occupy a space the size of Manhattan. The three main sites and sights are Angkor Wat, Angkor Thom, and Ta Prohm. Angkor Wat (Angkor is from the Sanskrit word *nagara* which means *city*. *Vot* is Cambodian for *pagoda* or *Buddhist shrine*) is first surrounded by a moat more than three and a half miles long with a 1/4 mile walkway over the moat and through a splendid portico of columns supporting a roof; it's like an enormous stone tunneled fence. The walk leads up to the entrance where huge blocks, comprised mainly of sandstone and also some limonite, fit together without cement, as straight and true as the horizon that welds the Cambodian sky and sea.

Does Your Meter Work?!

The brilliant and delicate carvings, thousands and thousands of characters, meticulously carved in bas-relief on a surrounding perimeter wall form a work of art totaling more than 17,000 square feet. Delicately whittled in precise, minute detail, the carvings dedicate stories to war and gods. From a network of hallways that shape the center, five majestic towers rise conically, patterned after the closed bud of a lotus flower, but look more like enormous rock asparagus tips. Angkor Wat is best seen at sundown when the sun aims its focused rays and gives the edifice a sacred, incandescent glow amid the darkening natural surroundings.

A stone fence two miles square with five gates of entry encloses Angkor Thom (Thom is from Thai *thom = great*, and the effect is indeed one of incredible size and ornate complexity). The centerpiece, *The Bayon,* is ablaze with faces. The haunting visage of Brahma sculpted on 20 extraordinary quadruply-faced towers soar all around. Moss and lichen add greenish-black hues to the washed white stone. The religious clarity of vision is mated to a generally clean landscaped setting.

Popular Ta Prohm, on the other hand, hasn't been cleaned up. The site demonstrates the phenomenal power of the jungle where elephantine trees have grown over walls and pushed through stone. In breathtaking dimensions, roots wider than telephone poles wrap themselves around structures like boa constrictors on their prey. Titanic roots tentacle down agonizingly, slowly strangling and swallowing its victim, a building or fence. Or the trees are giant candles, the roots dripping and cooling like melted wax.

The Western viewer feels overwhelmed, as when seeing the Egyptian Pyramids. In each place, one is puzzled by the simplest of questions: how a supposedly ancient culture could conceive of moving, and carving, the sheer amount and size of stone, then raising the works to such heights and symmetries. This is the architecture of genius combined with the organizational ability of brilliant rulers.

Of how hideous the Khmer Rouge were, Angkor Wat couldn't be more opposite on the astonishing scale. The two poles are so far apart, Cambodia fascinates the visitor to examine everything in between: whether to celebrate mankind for its incredible abilities, or loathe it for its shocking primitiveness.

Presently, plaques and signs dot the area recognizing foreign governments, NGO's, benevolent societies, and individual donors for their contributions toward the tremendous amount of work completed to clear the jungle and refurbish the crumbled portions. Unfortunately, treasure seekers steal statues and carvings to sell on the world market. Even more disturbing, collectors condone the pirates by paying for these treasures.

The benefit of walking between structures - albeit far in tropical heat - is the chance to hobnob with the locals. Farmers, students, and children with such purity and openness are as moving as the ruins. Their caution, especially the children's, disintegrates by simply smiling and saying hello. The youngsters laugh and giggle and shy-out over nothing. They dance and sing, queer out by their friends ribbing, run away, then just as quickly run straight back looking for more fun. The innocent happiness of youth is irrefutably evident in Cambodia.

For the layperson, Angkor Wat is a place to come and simply be. Marvel through your own eyes at what it offers and relish whatever part of the package that suits your personal taste. Is it the sheer size, the perfect carvings, the flawless construction, the might of the jungle, the placidity, Angkor Wat's poise and presence, or a combination of two or more? Poets and historians do their best to assemble the words to provide a satisfactory image of Angkor Wat's splendor, but words are a second-choice vehicle to replace a personal eyewitness account. Some spend a week at Angkor Wat, others a month. And yet, how many people have heard of it?

CAMBODIA, SMILES AND SKULLS

During the drive from the airport into Phnom Penh, something seemed peculiar; something I couldn't let go of that didn't add up. I dumped my stuff off, cleaned up a bit, and went exploring. As I skipped across the street, the source of my disquiet became clear. Most vehicles, including our taxi, were right-hand drive as in the U.K., but operate on the right side of the road as in North America. Things happen for a reason. Stay tuned.

Phnom Penh gets its name from Cambodian *phnom, mountain* or *hill,* and *penh, full* or traditionally known as *Mountain of Plenty*. Plenty of heat and dust. Absent is the polluted blue air found in other big Asian cities but a perpetual haze of dust lingers. Only the main roads resemble a hard surface. The side streets, neglected over the years, have crumbled into gravel and fine, arid silt.

In the Khmer language, Pol Pot means *Brother Number One*. His real name was *Saloth Sar*. Gruesome, dreadfully unmistakable signs of the ravages of his war still dot the streets. Shrapnel scars instead of eyes, rickety wheelchairs, one-legged people on makeshift crutches, and prosthetic limbs as simple as a stovepipe substituting for a leg complete with a wooden disc as a foot.

Soldiers, some lightly armed with M-16's and AK-47's, others in full battle gear, talked and laughed in groups like players of a football team waiting for the team bus. Cocky male adolescents milled around me, touching my bag and grabbing at my arm, smiling and saying hello. I didn't know what their actions meant, what they wanted, or how to take it. Were they dangerous or friendly? Would my sidestepping anger them? Are they more scared of me than I am of them? I felt my composure challenged. Was I happy that I'd arrived to see all this? I didn't know. Nasty fact stared me in the face, that I knew.

The King's Palace faced a busy thoroughfare and a riverfront park. Barricades otherwise surrounded the walled-off complex. My meanderings around town found me on a deserted street in the rear area of the grounds. Drawn by the distant action at the front of the palace, I decided to go for it. A few steps later, from behind a tree, stepped an inexperienced looking soldier with an experienced looking AK-47. He used body language to inquire of my destination. I pointed down the empty street to the front of the palace, and with a wave, he refused access. He pointed out directions for me to skirt around by using the next street over. I shrugged, retreated ten steps, and in the opposite direction, he joined a newly appeared colleague.

Plotting my next move, I studied the map of Phnom Penh in my guidebook. The two servicemen watching clapped their hands and waved me up. I put the book into my bag, zippered it shut, and wandered over.

"Where you go?" the other, older soldier quizzed in English.

"Up to the other side of the palace," I pointed.

"What you have?" He referred to my bag.

Why did he want to know? Was this a robbery? Feeling quite outgunned on this empty street, I didn't want him to see my camera, money, or documents pouch. Rebels had stormed the Japanese embassy in Peru two weeks ago. Was I to become an international incident?

Ample times in the past, in jams, albeit without assault rifles visible, I've successfully jabbered off in English, talking too quickly for others to understand. Usually, they're incapable of understanding and end the conversation straightaway. To exploit losing face in Asia is dirty pool - and a heckuva hole card.

I began blathering.
"Oh-in-here-I've-got-a-few-things-that-I-carry-with-me-because-I-don't-want-to-leave-anything-at-the-hotel (pointing in some direction) because-it's-better-to-take-everything-with-me (inhale) I've-got-my-camera-and-some-other-things-that....

They both squinted their eyes and tilted their heads trying to comprehend. The older soldier mimed holding a book and turning the pages.

"My book? You want to see my book?" I laughed.

"Book, book," they laughed in unison, looking at each other to confirm the other was laughing too.

I carefully dipped my hand into my bag, felt around until touching the book, and pulled it out. They flipped a couple pages, and handed it back. They permitted passage through the original route requested and I buggered off without hesitation. Their curiosity couldn't resist, and my international incident was much ado about nothing, but Cambodia's spookiness really kick-started my heart.

The palace entrance was closed off and heavily guarded. A truck filled with soldiers zoomed by and, to my surprise, one of their hats blew off and landed at my feet. I picked it up to give back, fully expecting to see brake lights and hear screeching tires. No one signaled the driver to stop and the truck, full of cackling and waving servicemen, disappeared around a bend.

I looked about. No one saw or if they did, they didn't care. I stuffed the officially badged olive green baseball cap into my bag and ambled on.

I looked in on some street vendors. Usually it's more of the same old victuals except this day they peddled deep-fried whole birds a little smaller than a Cornish hen and when I say whole, I mean whole, not counting the feathers. Also on the menu were deep-fried grasshoppers about the size of a shotgun shell and deep-fried cockroaches almost as big. I decided to save my money and appetite for later and settled for a photograph of the bugs.

A shirtless man wearing grubby pants and flip-flops, twentysomething, in a park across the street, stood over an infant who shuffled and waved his hands as children that age do. The man leaned on a single crutch, his left leg blown off just below the knee. Furtively, I let out the full 300 mm zoom lens, believing the distance separating us enough cover, and snapped off two frames. With his radar beamed in, he scooped up the child in one arm and began hobbling over to my position with the same hand out that bore the kid. I walked the opposite way, creating distance between us, him calling "money, money." I felt shame, fear, dishonor. Was taking a photo turning him into a cheap, peek-a-boo midway act? Did I owe him money? Could it be said he was exploiting his debilitation? I didn't know and kept on walking.

The Silver Pagoda, an attention-grabbing tourist stop when it's open, houses solid gold Buddhas trimmed with huge diamonds and other precious stones. The floor is covered with 5329 tiles of silver, each weighing 1.125kg. Photography not permitted. Why hadn't the Khmer Rouge looted it? Was a conscience in there somewhere?

Does Your Meter Work?!

Ten miles outside Phnom Penh is the most famous Killing Fields, those of Choeung Ek. A terrific guy named Leat (LEE-AT) guided me through the area on his Honda 50. The haunting image of what transpired offsets a lack of structure. Approximately 17,000 people were killed and buried in 129 mass graves. Workers exhumed over 8,000 remains from 86 graves, then collected and arranged the skulls by sex and age into a glass stupa as a memorial. Leat pointed out the gaping holes and cuts in the skulls where hammers or axes bludgeoned the victims.

On the floor of the stupa sit rusted garden shears, hoes, hammers, saws, and leg chains used as instruments of torture and death. The part of the leaf that grows near the trunk of palm oil trees are stiff with sharp, serrated edges resembling organic Swede saws, the Khmer Rouge tool of decapitation. Khmer Rouge held children and women by the feet and Leat pointed out the separate trees where the victims' heads were smashed. Small dugouts survive with bits of cloth, bones, and teeth scattered about. With killing fields and mass graves throughout the country, estimations differ that anywhere from one to two million people perished through execution and maltreatment.

In Phnom Penh city, a prison and torture chamber, originally a school, is now the Museum of Genocide. The classrooms became jails. Slaves constructed tiny cells of brick and mortar, then secured chains into the floor. A wall shows rows and rows of black-and-white mug shots with numbers on the chests of the soon-to-be-massacred. Another wall of photos unmask the inhumanity, their bodies now shown in assorted horizontal poses of death.

Leat patiently explained that he was 17 when Pol Pot terminated lawful studying. Conscripted to the south, Leat worked in the rice fields for three years and eight months from 5:30 a.m. to 9 at night. Twice a day he was fed watery rice.

"No meat! No meat! Only rice! No vegetables! Only rice!" Finally, laughing to break his tension, he said, "Pol Pot crazy, Pol Pot crazy!"

Most remarkable about Cambodia? The pervasive gaiety on each visage, despite the history, despite the pain, despite the losses. The adults initially stare with an unsettling fear and apprehension, but by smiling first, life gushes to their faces in return. The children explode with immediate unsolicited joy, grinning from temple to temple, waving delightedly, and bursting, "Hello! Hello!" Simply waving back with a smile or a reciprocal "hello" inspires torrential giggles.

Leat, my chauffeur, guide, friend, and Cambodian encyclopedia has the highest ratio of smile per square inch in the history of faces. He never let me down, or tried to weasel an extra nickel.

"Leat, why are the cars' steering wheels different?"

In not so many words, he unraveled the mystery. Cars drive in the right lane because the French colonized Cambodia. Left hand drive cars come in from Vietnam, also a former colony of France. Right hand drives are smuggled/bribed in from Thailand which, along with Malaysia, motors on the left side.

"Where did you get enough money to buy this motorcycle?"

"My uncle live Canada."

"Really. Do you know where?"

"Addamootoo."

"Addamootoo?"

"Yeah, in Canada."

"Edmonton?"

"Yeah, Addamootoon."

"That's where I'm from!"

"Tell hello my uncle!"

MOC BAI

Transportation choices from Phnom Penh, Cambodia to Saigon (Ho Chi Minh City) were either to fly or go on land. Overland, in turn, had two alternatives: bus or shared taxi to the border. Moc Bai was the point of entry at the south end of Vietnam where taxis destined for Saigon waited on the other side. A restaurant arranged foreigner taxis, $23 for four passengers. Pieces of paper tacked to a bulletin board held room for four names and the date of departure.

Leat, my motorcycle chauffeur for the previous three days, presented a Cambodian taxi opportunity at $5 per person, cramming in six passengers. Since my declared date of entry to Vietnam offered no foreigner taxis, I had agreed. The night before leaving, on the board, a notice with my date materialized with a space remaining. A disappointed Leat missed out on a commission, a development which did nothing to extinguish his Hall-of-Fame smile. I bade him farewell and thanked him for his help.

In the morning, our fourth person couldn't get out of bed. Three of us agreed to split the $23 and set off. The road, with two-way traffic, was a lane and a half wide filled with cars, trucks, motorcycles, bicycles, pedestrians, playing children, farm animals, ox carts, bursting buses, and pot-holes. Actually, more like cauldron-holes.

Our driver must have had the most muscular thumb on the planet because he rarely took it off the horn, even continuing during the scarce stretches without life. We approached an object. It was well in the distance and stationary. Not sure of it's identity, I suppose, and unwilling to chance losing an opportunity to blast any candidates, his relentless thumb laid on the horn. It was a rock.

A rooster tried strutting across on his own time. Without a final flurry of feathered flying he narrowly missed becoming part of the undercarriage. After being hatched and raised in a third world country, you'd think he'd know the streets weren't his barnyard back yard. There was only one question...why did that chicken cross the road? Even the dour driver found it funny.

The 90 miles took all of five hours. Weary legs stuttered onto the dusty road, and a few deep breaths cleared the carbon monoxide that had seeped through the seats and into my lungs. We wobbled the final few hundred yards to the border. Why wouldn't the driver take us all the way?

The Moc Bai border crossing into Vietnam makes a great picture. A pastel blue sign, a wide, sweeping arc over the first building says VIETNAM. Policemen, in their distinctive olive-green uniforms, flat-top hat with a bright red band, and a disinterested look about their carriage says communism. Also, just as distinctive, is a sign saying, in English, NO PICTURES.

My Swiss and Canadian traveling companions and I passed through the first two checkpoints without incident but at the third, Christopher, the Swiss, hit a Vietnamese brick wall. Christopher had originally flown into Saigon and had indicated on his passport he would fly out when leaving. He subsequently had decided on a trip to Cambodia for Angkor Wat. Before leaving Saigon, he asked for Moc Bai departure and re-entry to be marked in his passport. Vietnamese Immigration furnished a special stamp assuring him it was sufficient as he had a triple entry visa. He obviously left Vietnam but on this day, trying to return, the customs officer unconditionally turned him away. "Moc Bai" must be stamped. Now, his alternative was to take a taxi, alone, back to Phnom Penh and re-apply for a new visa meaning 42 bucks, plus transport, plus the expense of living for four days waiting on bureaucracy, plus his parents -- career diplomats -- waiting in Saigon for his return. How was everyone to communicate between two countries that officially hated each other?

In a remarkable award-winning performance, he played his last card: grovel piteously. Not without sympathy, Rob and I stood by for more than an hour to show solidarity but, I'm afraid, there is yet to be built an instrument sufficiently sensitive to measure this officer's indifference. Christopher followed the officer around like a puppy pleading for some understanding. Occasionally, Christopher directed a grin and a wink our way then retumbled deeply into his sorrowful monologue.

Rob and I did our best to horn-swoggle the other officers with arguments leaning towards the first officer's inability to understand English and that if the second officer, whose vastly superior skills in English we took huge pains to point out, could only slide over and straighten up this whole misunderstanding, everyone would be positively peachy. This strategy went over like a lead zeppelin so Rob and I downgraded our argument to Saigon Immigration had guaranteed everything was in order and that Rob's and my personal endorsements were as good as gold. Eventually Christopher convinced us to go on. A couple more hours of begging were worth his time but I have a feeling he had no luck.

So after years of fascination about Vietnam (Viet is the name of a former principality of southern China and nam means south) because of the war, I was here. The taxis on this side, private cars with no meters, played hardball on their $20 price to Saigon. Rob tendered $16, ineffectually appealing that our numbers had dwindled to two therefore diluting our buying power. Vietnam knows not the concept of seat-sales.

We were both starved and not unhappy to trade the bargaining table for the dining table; all a bluff and part of the cat and mouse game ceaselessly played.

We enjoyed a chicken leg, rice, fresh salad, and bananas for $1.50; the food quality was definitely a step up from Cambodia. Another foreigner came along to share the transportation costs and the hollow maneuvering on price ended.

The wide, smooth highway into Saigon was packed. During the 60 miles, the stream of people never ended, motorcycles everywhere. One lay beside a chalk outline of a body. A nude lady walked along the shoulder waving her arms in the air above witchy, matted, and scattered hair, talking to no one in particular, and reshuffling the toys in her attic.

"Your date's here," I informed my Canuck companion. Then I asked something that had been on my mind. "Did you think about a bribe back at the border?"

"I wondered but wasn't sure."

"Me either."

In Saigon, the driver commanded one more dollar, igniting a big screaming match on the sidewalk. No one in any country had been this aggressive or rapacious. If this had been day one in Asia, maybe we pay. Instead, we walked away, wondering aloud if we had missed something and really owed him.

Does Your Meter Work?!

I had no way of knowing what a harbinger of things to come this introduction to Vietnam would be. Stay tuned for more on the wacky world of Vietnam.

TEACHING ENGLISH IN ASIA

After eight months as an English teacher in Taiwan, I'd saved my money and had begun tramping around Asia. Five countries later, and a lifetime of wishing to brave Vietnam, I found myself in Saigon where, for 50,000 dong ($1=12,000VND) per night, I found a clean, dilapidated character room. A real fixer-upper. The desk lady spoke decent English.

"Do you know where I can teach English?" I asked her.

"Mister Glenn, he from Canada, he live same floor you, room 405, he teacher."

"Is he in?"

"He no here."

"If I leave him a note, can you give it to him?"

"No problem."

Big smile. Rotten teeth. Dentistry is THE growth industry in this part of the world.

"Mr. Glenn," a Canadian named Glenn Loewen, left a note to meet in the lobby the next day at 1.

Right on time, Mr. Glenn, a generous-in-spirit, middle-aged man, provided the address for his school, and marked its location on the city map in my guidebook.

"Ask for a lady named Kim-Le. She'll smile the chrome off a bumper," was the only advice he offered.

During my interview with Miss Kim-Le, I blazed with all my guns: previous teaching experience in a "rich" country, rudimentary Mandarin skills, and rusty French. She offered nine dollars an hour, one more than their usual starting rate.

"I will call you at your hotel when I have a class."

We shook hands, used up the world's quota in thank you's until there was no chrome left on my bumper, and I walked home. The desk girl handed me a piece of paper along with my key.

"You school call. Miss Kim-Le. You have class two days later. Congratulations, Mr. Jim."

I ran into Mr. Glenn later that night in a bar, and bought him a beer in thanks. An American named Don, law school graduate, concert violinist, and pompous as hell joined our discussion. He had been in Vietnam for a year or so, uncommitted to chasing the American Dream. He informed me of his school, and how to find it. The next day I tracked it down, chatted with the school's director, another American more self-important than Don, and decided to work for Kim-Le.

And so it goes when teaching in Asia. The ostensible required teaching qualifications total two: proof of a degree, which I had but never pulled out of my bag, and to be a native English speaker, which never stopped all the Western Europeans who spoke English so well. Anything extra can get you an extra buck an hour. The unspoken rule is: Caucasians need only apply, however the stance on ABC's (American Born Chinese, also known as 'bananas,' yellow on the outside, white on the inside) has softened.

Teaching in Asia was a challenge and it wasn't a challenge. Nor was it necessarily about education. The school used a textbook but few teachers, myself included, made lesson plans or engaged in outside the classroom preparation. To be pedantic was the kiss of death. Discussing grammar and structure was lip service.

The greatest challenge was to be entertaining. The students reported that they liked you, which allowed more hours, and dollars, to become available.

The students, who paid to be near foreigners and glean exposure to the other side, spent the majority of each night's two hours speaking Vietnamese unless called upon because "it's too hard to say it in English." "But isn't that why we are here and why you spend all this money?" produced a smile and not much else.

On the first day of a new class, if enrolment was eighteen students, then maybe, if lucky, three showed up with an English/Vietnamese dictionary. I would lay out my usual script persuading everyone to either bring his or hers or buy one. Decent Oxford dictionaries were abundant for a few dollars. Excuses alternated from "You're our dictionary" to "I forgot."

As I established my existence around the school, I was asked to substitute for one class, a Friday evening. Twenty or so expressionless faces asked the same stock questions: Where are you from? How old are you? Are you married? How long have you been in Vietnam? Can you speak Vietnamese? Where do you stay? How much salary do you get?

47

Does Your Meter Work?!

I escaped to the teacher's room after the protracted two hours expecting to see gallows erected. Before leaving the building however, I was appointed their new teacher by Miss Kim-Le, freshly informed by her paying customer's report. I shook my head all the way home, changed out of the obligatory shirt and tie, and met Mr. Glenn.

"I know, Mr. Jim," he said soothingly while ordering two beers, "It happens all the time ... and the other way around, too. Don't forget, there's a teacher who has suddenly lost a class."

Two nights later, Sunday evening, three students from the class, with a present in hand, were waiting at my hotel for me to arrive, and would I like to come around by motorcycle for the evening? They politely requested that I change to trousers from shorts and then we could go. Over some wonderful soup that I wasn't permitted to help pay for, they asked the most intimate, personal questions about past love lives and future plans.

Then, sure enough, just when I felt other classes were going loftily, I'd be replaced. The administration would be sticky sweet with good news, and colder than frozen carbon dioxide with bad tidings.

Over time, I honed my teaching strategy into doing whatever I did in class and let whoever was going to get whatever they were going to get out of it. I didn't know the most effective way to reach and teach the students. I established a faith that somewhere, somehow, someone in that sea of blank faces was getting something out of the lesson.

Mr. Glenn and I became good friends. We dissected our jobs (like all teachers seem to do) and the English language ad nauseam. One of our favorite philosophical confrontations stemmed from how to speak to our students. Mr. Glenn debated that if the teacher sanitized and watered down the conversation, the students would inevitably fail in a real-life, on-the-street conversation. If the teacher spoke baby talk, then the students wouldn't be prepared.

I viewed the classroom as a laboratory and a sanctuary. A language is learned one concept, formula, phrase, or word at a time, spinning an interconnecting web as slowly or quickly as the student's talents and desires dictated. If the teacher skipped stages and leapt to the top of the ability mountain, students became confused, then dizzy, until finally lost.

The Confucian philosophy doesn't lend itself to training its protégés to learn in concepts, instead preferring a slavish devotion to the teacher and rote learning. An all-too-typical conversation went like this:

Mr.Glenn (to his friend): Hello, Mr. Nguyen, how are you?

Mr. Nguyen: Fine thank you, and you?

Mr. Glenn: I'm well, thank you. This is my friend, Mr. Jim.

Mr. Nguyen: Hello (extending a hand). What's your name?

The first thought was "He didn't understand the English word 'Jim'." However, Vietnamese understand "Mister" because every male was referred to as "Mister (insert name here)." Females were "Miss (insert name here)." The stock response, "Hello. What's your name?" was robotic, learned by rote through regular school, then night school, summer school, and tutors.

To be fair, English contains more words than any other language. Comprehending by listening for vocabulary is crucial. Sometimes, listening for context is required when, for example, homophones are used. Homophones are words that sound the same, have different spellings, and different meanings. The words "know" and "no" confuse. If the teacher asks, "Do you know what day is today?" the student may understand, "Do you 'no' what day is today?" The student, not listening for context, thinks the "know" means "no", as in not. The student misunderstands the entire sentence and responds with a preposterous answer from left field. Then, a confused teacher says, "No" because the exercise is already off its rails.

Vietnamese has simpler grammar rules, therefore the student may think the teacher is saying, "Know" as in, "Yes, I know." The two parties eye each other, waiting for the next move. Nothing happens, the teacher is flustered, the student loses face, momentum is lost, the lesson stalls.

Another scenario has the teacher saying "I know you like English" that may come across to a student as, "I no like you(r) English." A major misunderstanding looms because the student will clam up in fear of continuing to disappoint the teacher.

Another great conversation:

Foreigner (on the telephone): Is so and so there?

Non-speaker: He not here.

Foreigner: Oh, he's not there?

Non-speaker: Yes. (As in agreement, "Yes, he's not here." In English, to agree, the response is, "No" as in "No, he's not here.")

Foreigner: Oh, he is there?

Non-speaker: No.

Foreigner: Oh, he's not there.

Non-speaker: Yes.

Foreigner: Oh, he is there?

Non-speaker: No.

Foreigner: Wait a second, is he there or not?

Non-speaker: No.

Foreigner: I thought you said he was there.

Non-speaker: Yes, he's not here.

Foreigner: Oh, forget it. <Click>

One of the greatest sins within Oriental cultures is losing face. Teachers wondered "Why don't they just say 'no' or 'I don't know'?" Students contended with suffocating pressure that their English will be not just acceptable nor all right nor adequate or even exceptional; only perfection would satisfy. The safer route was to say nothing rather than risk the ridicule of peers ruthless in their scorn. Childish memories were short as the loudest laughers turned into instant bowls of quivering jelly when asked to answer better.

The anniversary celebrating the fall of Saigon was dubbed "Liberation Day." As this holiday approached, I used the opportunity to initiate conversations in class and, for my own curiosity, investigate how the Saigonese felt about losing the war.

"What will you do for the holiday?" I asked a twentysomething lady.

"I will be happy for Liberation Day."

"Why do you call it 'Liberation' Day?"

"Because this day is when we are not a colony of America."

"Are you glad the North won the war?"

"No, I don't like the Communists."

"Do you wish the Americans won the war?"

"If America won we are not communist country."

Does Your Meter Work?!

"But the communists 'liberated' South Vietnam."

Smiles and giggles broke out. I tried shaking the tree by branching off into a discussion between the differences of democracy and communism but it never took root. One teacher apparently sprouted the same discussion, which resulted in a special teachers' meeting. A mysterious, cross-armed, sober-faced jasper whose tie was far too big for his suit attended, where the administration ordered, with canyonesque grins, to abstain from such lessons.

A good teacher affects eternity
- Chinese Proverb

Balancing out the personal swings in disappointment and puzzlement were the students to whose lives a difference was made. Of the hundreds taught, only four or five became true friends. The pupils who opened up and made themselves available to friendship with "the foreigner" became very close very quickly. Every teacher had her/his own devoted, warm relationships that were true and from the heart. The special students were known because it was their motorcycle the teacher rode when the group went out, or the chat took longer with them in the stairwell while the class remained in waiting.

The look on their faces in class said the message was finding its way in, not in a gooey, star-struck manner, but in the meta-awareness way we know we're on to something when we're on to something. It was true, pure, and undiluted, not to be forgotten in a lifetime.

Their loyalty was unparalleled. They would walk through walls of fire in friendship, always a guaranteed "yes" because of a genuine desire to please, harnessing all their might and fury to try and make your life better. Such as waiting to drive you home, collecting their allies in class to take you out, all expenses paid, or seek out what your needs happened to be at the moment and how could they help. Making that difference in just one person's life makes the whole escapade worthwhile.

Judgement day approached; I'd had enough and wanted to continue traveling. My week's notice startled the school and jump-started a leak that a second building of classrooms full of shiny, eager faces was to open within the month, putting teachers in short supply. Kim-Le used all her available charm to convince me to stay, then she finally resigned to my imminent departure.

A small farewell of lunch and pastries with the staff and a sweet note that read, "A nightingale won't sing while it's in a cage" cut the cord. Students held parties and I carried present after present home. Unfortunately, everything except a notebook was useless to my traveling needs. Mr. Glenn relished in his windfall of ties, dress shirts, and ornaments.

A couple of days later, Saigon was done, and disappearing out the back window of a northbound bus.

Being born a native English speaker is equivalent to winning a lottery before you've bought a ticket. You carry, without lifting a finger, a portable skill that millions kill themselves to gain and for some, quite literally, their lives depend upon getting. Although venturing to another country to work is a big dare, see it as an extraordinary opportunity, with the broadest definition of extraordinary. In time, after your traveling afar is over, and you have suddenly found yourself back on home turf, you'll miss the new worlds you discovered, even when you conclude that your unremarkable little hometown had been one of the world's best-kept secrets.

SAIGON BARS & CAFES

The bars and cafes of Saigon grant their own kind of entertainment and provide the stage to dive deeper into the Vietnamese psyche. A student of mine, a bright, privileged 19-year-old, intended to study in America. Over a beer, he picked my brain for some insight into life on the other side of the ditch. I told him that in the States, he could do, say, and think anything he wanted. He said, "Yes, I want to go to America but too much freedom is not good."

A mid-twenties Vietnamese male asked if I'd been to the north. "Not yet but will make my way eventually," I answered. He didn't like the north (north meaning Hanoi) because of too many Viet Cong. He hated the VC. I asked why. He started briefly then, with an angry, fearful look, asked why I wanted to know, wondered if I was VC, then took his beer and moved to another part of the bar.

A friendly group of young Vietnamese guys sat at a sidewalk café hangout on Friday and Saturday evenings, drinking and eating and telling fish stories. They spoke nice English and always had a glass and a nibble for their invited. One particularly fluent 31 year old remembered the U.S. soldiers as kind, always giving out treats and playing with the kids. Vietnamese families lived well and contentedly until the fall of Saigon. After, his father, who had taught mathematics in French, could only teach in Vietnamese.

Today, Hanoi ships managers to Saigon to take up the best jobs at already successful businesses. He doesn't discount another civil war except underground movements can't get together and agree to become strong enough. The end of the Cold War has dried up any resources towards that end.

Many of us English teachers swigged and smoked at a little coffee shop next to the school owned by a husband and wife team. The husband, who spoke masterful English, had worked closely with the Americans as a captain in the South Vietnamese Army. Husky and crew cut, he easily quoted Shakespeare, Lincoln, and poetry. Amiable and chatty, he remembered everyone's name on first meeting. For the life of him, he couldn't understand how his side could have lost the war.

"We had piles of the best weapons on Earth left behind by America. We were soldiers and all we had to do was pick them up and fight but everyone just turned around and ran away. The Vietnamese officers, instead of commanding the men, used their contacts to run away to America and left their own people to die."

"How do you feel about those officers today?"

Embittered lava blasted from his eyes, "I hate them, I hate them all. They were cowards and if they came back here, I'd kill them."

He spent seven years in a re-education camp after the fall of Saigon. It could have been much less but "I was a trouble-maker."

"I work here but my boyfriend doesn't know," said a bar waitress. "I work here to pay for my older brother to go to university and younger brother to go to high school."

"What about you?"

"I study English. My boyfriend will marry me."

"You can't go to school?"

"I have a boyfriend with a good job. My brothers are men, they are important."

"Aren't you important?"

"I will have a husband," she snickered in a manner that suggested our conversation, plus all the reasoning behind it, was dumb, "That's enough."

The same waitress knew I was looking to move from my hotel. We rendezvoused in the afternoon, then she guided me to the house of her friend who had a room for rent. Rare is the Vietnamese woman who will be seen with a foreign male under the glare of daylight. Cyclo drivers turned and stared while driving blindly down the street. A few spat comments.

The room was too small. Outside, she accepted my disapproval, which I found peculiar. I expected the hard sell.

"What we tell my friend?"

"Tell her I didn't like it enough, too small."

"No, I can't say. I tell her you say the room too hot."

"Oh, yeah? Why?"

"That's better, then everyone happy."

All the staff from the same bar were extra nice. They adopted me as their teacher.

Does Your Meter Work?!

"How you say this in English?"
"Napkin."
"And this?"
"Coaster."
"What this in English?"
"Bottle."
"What this?"
"Peanuts."

After each new word, the staff would parrot my repeats until my "yes" signaled their successful enunciation. Not a soul could hit the "t" sound in peanuts. Articulate the word "peanuts" with heartfelt clarity, and omit the "t" sound. Imagine a full bar of foreigners looking over their shoulders at a circle of five or six Vietnamese young men and women reproducing their new word loudly, over and over, nodding approvingly at their classmates' apparent success.

And what comes around goes around. Many languages in Asia are tonal. Adding a different inflection, or tone, to the same sound changes the meaning. Mandarin has four tones, Vietnamese seven. A favorite student attempted to teach me, "No MSG please" in Vietnamese. He held his tact as long as possible, and then howled in laughter. The vocabulary was easy enough but apparently my English mouth was programmed to hit the tone to request "No boils on my ass, please."

My colleague, Mr.Glenn, had a student whose wife was a singer. The husband invited Mr. Glenn to check her out and I tagged along. The student had warned Mr. Glenn not to pay any cover charge. We took a taxi because they always used their meter, we refused a couple of loitering guys asking for 50,000 VND admissions, and went inside the dark, steamy, smoky ballroom. The customers, of all ages, were dressed in gowns and suits. Tables celebrated birthdays and anniversaries with cakes and presents. We ordered a drink and the band came back. The lady pulled up on stage to polite applause. Colored lights flooded the stage and some wicked guitar licks resumed the party. A bit hefty, an Oriental Aretha Franklin, the wife belted out in flawless, unaccented English CCR's "Proud Mary," The Doors "LA Woman," and three or four other rock 'n roll classics as she rhythmically danced Latin steps in perfect time. The couples swished and swayed in each other's arms to ballroom steps out of a pre-Happy Days epoch as the lady's booming, kick-ass voice pulled the paint off the walls.

The music was far too loud for Mr. Glenn and I to consult. We displayed our delighted surprise through facial calisthenics of lifted eyebrows, bugged out eyes, and a dropping of the chin without breaking the seal of the lips, then an approving nod before reaching for a refreshment on the table as an excuse to break eye contact and resume taking in the show.

We rocked along until the final number, and the party broke up as quickly as it started. Once at our table, she was shier than expected. At first, I thought I was witnessing another episode of saving face by her humble reserve.

"She doesn't speak English," her husband informed us.

SAIGON STREETS

The streets of Saigon teem with people, noises, and smells like no other city in Asia. "What's in front is more important than what's behind" pilots the vehicles through the streets. The proportion of motorcycles to four-wheeled vehicles is, maybe, 200 to 1. Consistent with the Law of Natural Selection, the right-of-way totem pole starts at the big transport trucks, then buses, smaller trucks, pick-ups, cars, cyclos, motorcycles, and finally, pedestrians. To lane change, anyone beside or behind yields unless they're bigger. A vehicle traveling straight through an intersection yields to another cutting in while making their right-hand turn, without looking, of course, unless they're bigger. Perhaps 'yield' confuses by implying rules. Better than yield is "miss."

The evolution of the street forced the previously outlined principles into the only pragmatic fashion to get anywhere. No affliction of "road rage" nor the outlook of "you drive like a jerk but me, I'm in a hurry" appears to exist. Either they're all jerks or all in a hurry ... another in the long list of puzzles I never figured out.

One rule, established by either tacit agreement or an unspoken course of events is the right turn for large four-wheeled vehicles. Safety and logic dictate that when fashioning a right hand turn, move to the far right (curb) lane, signal right, and turn into the perpendicular right hand (curb) lane. To turn right in Vietnam, the signal light is thoughtfully activated, a swamper in the passenger seat warns the motorcycles of a right-hand turn with a downward waving of his hand, and the vehicle turns right -- from the far left lane. Go figure. If you can understand it, that makes one of us.

Like spiders with a freshly spun web, cops sit on the other side of major intersections waiting for traffic light violators. The rule of thumb for payoffs is half the official fine on the ticket. Price also depends on what clothes the offending driver wears and the quality of his motorcycle. An affluent appearance translates into a higher kickback.

When the street is no longer the focus, there's an obstacle course called the sidewalk to manage. Bicycles, motorcycles, vendors, chairs, cyclos, garbage, and pooches barking out both ends litter the sidewalks. The curb is the only place to walk. A driver on a motorcycle cuts in front, brakes suddenly, kicks the stand down, and walks away in a flash, leaving you to suddenly stop and side step. The driver looks straight on, maybe picking his teeth, or more accurately, picking his nose, aloof to his rudeness. I constantly speculated if he really didn't know how inconsiderate he was or purely couldn't care.

Two male youths sped by on a motorcycle and tried to grab the day bag slung over my shoulder once. Fortunately they were going too fast for the passenger bandit to get a good grip. They did a 360-degree turnaround at the corner and took off. One foreigner recounted a friend's story. A Vietnamese tried to steal his bag. The friend started beating on him. A crowd gathered and the friend suddenly thought, "Uh-oh, I'm surrounded." The locals finished the punishment, held up the perpetrator, instructed, "You have one more shot." then took him away to the police.

A hand is always out trying to pander or peddle something. Vendors of all ages, some as young as two, toil the streets selling cigarettes, gum, candies, roses, lighters, watches, fans, anything that may make money. Under the danger of a beating, many are forbidden to return home until everything is sold.

The kids recognize no and move on but too many adults cannot. Weeks of refusals can pass before the vendors realize that "No, thank-you" means "No, thank-you." Then "No thanks." Then "No." Then "Please go away." Then "NO." Then "GET LOST." Then "FUCK OFF, WHY CAN'T YOU UNDERSTAND!? I DON'T WANT OR NEED A LIGHTER IN THE SHAPE OF A PORSCHE THAT LIGHTS WHEN YOU PUSH ON ITS HOOD!"

"You are all so rich, so rich," they exclaim.

With no meters, all rides are negotiated. Before I learned market rates, I argued so many times with motorcycle-taxis and cyclo drivers who lost no sleep ripping off fares. They seemed to want a savior, expecting to go for a ride to nowhere so I could pass on my money, which would never be enough anyway.

I walked into a small store flush with jeans. The only sign in the store read "80,000 VND", written in felt pen on a piece of cardboard among folded jeans on a display table. The two salesmen saw me enter and move towards this area. Their pace picked up, and they arrived just ahead of me in time to drop the sign on its face. I asked how much the jeans were, they spoke three or four sentences together, and arrived at the quote.

"130,000," they announced.

I picked up the sign and asked what's what.

"No," was all they could say.

I spun the sign at them like a frisbee, hitting one in the chest, and called them "big liars" in Vietnamese before walking out.

A quantity of pot the size of a cigarette package runs about $3, relentlessly brokered by cyclo drivers. Most people buy it OTBC -- Over The Bar Counter. Establishments sell grass openly and the customers (Vietnamese rarely smoke) roll and lazily smoke reefers like a cigarette. Their eyes hang to their knees, sparkling beneath pillowed eyelids. I felt embarrassed.

But the sky generally stays put. Every morning, like clockwork, I bought The Bangkok Post from a husband and wife team who sold newspapers and magazines from a piece of plywood on sawhorses set up in the street. Even though neither could speak English, each day they burst into huge smiles and placed gentle touches on my shoulder. If I was late, they always saved me a copy, accompanied with huge roars of laughter and pride at their customer service.

One morning, the police showed up early with scissors and cut out a disparaging article about the Vietnamese government. Mrs. Broadsheet was angry and heart-broken and so was I because that article would have been interesting to read. Then, after I definitely understood the situation, and it wasn't her fault, she broke into wild laughter and pulled my saved copy, still intact, from under a pile of other magazines. She danced a jig, rolled her chubby hips, and waved her hands in the air, saying again and again, "Poli, Poli (Police, Police)."

COIN CANDY CAPERS

I entered Vietnam overland from Cambodia and traveled to Saigon. The next day I found a job teaching English, and everything went so well, I decided to stay a while longer. My visa was soon to expire calling for a quick visa run flight to Bangkok. The problem was I had entered the country by car, and had indicated on the application form that I would exit the same way. The convenience of a flight was in doubt. The government ostensibly wants to keep track of its visitors.

Mr. Nghia, the owner of the school where I worked, promised he had a contact in the Immigration department who could finagle the red tape.

"No problem," he smiled.

As the final day of my visa approached and passed, Mr. Nghia never let up on his smile.

"We still wait. No problem, you will be O.K."

Finally, 12 days post-expiry, the papers came through.

"Take these papers and your passport to the Vietnam embassy in Bangkok. You will have no problem."

"What about my expired visa?"

"When you go through Customs at the airport, hide VND150, 000 ($13) in your passport. VND 200,000 is better, but 150,000 is enough. More importantly, smile. Always (he pulled up the corners of his mouth with his pointer fingers) BIG smile."

I'd been in country long enough to see a little coin-candy sweeten a few teeth. I felt ready.

A couple of days later at the airport, I queued in one of the three busy Immigration lines. The travelers in front of me slowly dwindled. My cash-carrot revved its engine within my documents. The thick yellow line on the floor seemed like the edge of a cornfield: if I cross it, the baksheesh will come. Today's pigeon, dressed in his perfect uniform and firm demeanor, waved me forward. My papers slid across the desk from one greased palm to another and the game was on.

The entire airport lit up from my smile. So beaming was this grin, the Aurora Borealis went on the list of North American imports. The officer flicked open my passport and crisp currency fell from inside the back cover. His eyes pleated on his startled face. He glanced up. A Geiger counter could now measure my smile. He flipped to the page that held my Vietnamese visa stamp. He checked the date on his watch. Now, his face ignited.

"No pay here!" he broadcast, "No give money me!"

I flushed.

"Shhhhhhhhhh, ya dope," my mind yelled back. My big Clint Eastwood scene collapsed to Don Knotts.

"Go downstair, pay money at desk for too long visa. No pay me," he blared again.

Gargantuan smile. On him! His patriotism to the job was one in a million.

I feigned a "huh" then an "oh, sorry" and slid past the people down a staircase to a table where a man sat, so bored his mother-in-law must have just left. I showed him my things, he wrote a receipt, and asked for a VND 90,000 penalty.

Back upstairs my hero waved me up through the pack.

"Sorry sir, no pay me," he hollered in gleeful practice of his English, uncertain though it was.

Big smiles by each of us.

He slapped down my exit stamp and I scurried to my plane bound for Thailand from where I returned the next evening.

SAIGON HOOKERS

The dysfunctional side of conservative, patriarchal, xenophobic Vietnamese society seems to create basically two kinds of girls in Vietnam. One is a prostitute and the other a poster girl for Acme Chastity Belts. Because the Vietnamese gossip endlessly, and ruthlessly, few "nice" girls are nervy enough to be seen with a foreign male, a shame because many Vietnamese women are picture perfect, the benchmark for sensitive and often sensual femininity. The elegant two-piece traditional Vietnamese dress, the Ao Dai (pronounced "ow - yai"), covers from the neck to the feet. The top that covers their slender forms is a tight fitting silk blouse, slit to the knee along the side of each thigh. Loose-legged slacks fit snugly in the derriere. The light, flowing silk teasingly catches and clings to delicate curves or, "covers everything and hides nothing." Even "non-working" women augment their allure with an innate, seductive look that leaves the foreign male with the feeling of getting laid at any moment. It is all thunder and no lightning. These beguiling, unattainable sirens only add to feelings of puzzlement.

Part of Vietnam's New Economy is the tourist ghetto in Saigon, Pham Ngu Lao (pronounced Fum New Lao) Street. The bars are the natural meeting point each evening for the foreigners working in country, hence faces become familiar in short order and the area becomes its own little village. When a new face shows itself, the hookers that hang in the bars are instantly in it, probing for fresh business. After the girls realize the latest cash cow gives no milk, especially the amount of milk the girls are milking, they relax or give up - but there's a 3-5 night breaking-in period.

Many hookers simply can't get over themselves. One not-so-attractive working lady proffered me every night for weeks on end with the same line, "You, me, we go hotel, 50 dollar." Lowering her bottom line to, say, ten bucks would score her, for sure, two to four tricks a night from the horny toads passing through town -- good money in a country where 50 dollars a month is the going rate for a real job, a full meal costs under a dollar, and a pair of custom-made shoes are around ten. One night as she approached, I readied myself for her bid. Instead, she took my empty bottle, wiped the table, and scrunched her eyes like it was my fault she was, ugh, working in a bar for three dollars a shift.

Another more attractive independent contractor mired in a bad spell of business complained more than usual one night.

"How much are you charging?" I asked.

She had a key chain with bills printed on plastic that slid over each other. She leafed through them starting at the $1. *Couldn't be that one*. She got to the five. *Cambodia price*. Ten. *We must be close*. Twenty. *You better be stopping here, girl*. Fifty. *Huh?* At the hundred, my sympathies ended. She then retreated to the fifty and said, "This one. Sometime this one" as she returned to the C-note.

"I think maybe that's your problem," I counseled. "You're very pretty, you're a nice lady and your English is good, but Vietnam is very cheap. I'm a foreigner, fifty is too much."

"No, no. Foreigner have much money, they no me give, I want to go to my house far from Saigon, know (see) my mother but…no money."

Then she went back to her other Achilles heel: roto-rooting her sinus cavities with her finger while sitting alone at the end of the bar. In her culture, public digging is a non-starter, but it kills the mood, and sale, rather quickly.

Another equally unappealing tart always in Bette Midler broad character was particularly forthright. Market value -- 20 bucks plus hotel. Up to her usual tricks, she waddled up to one of the barflies and fired her opening salvo. He'd had 1) a few pops and 2) enough of her, so he turned the tables and undercut her, a seat sale as it were.

"No, no, no, you pay <u>me</u>," he shot back. "You give me 10 dollars, we go hotel, I make you happy, you very happy, you feel soooo good, you pay me. Only 10 dollars!"

"Vietnam girl no pay! Girl in Vietnam NEVER pay! Only man pay in Vietnam!" she cried out in colossal affront. With incredulous stomps, she fled to one of her colleagues at the other end of the bar. The ally nodded and gasped sympathetically as she learned more details, for she had witnessed the man's audacity from afar. A sudden, unexpected rash of handshakes appeared before the affronter's eyes from a number of strangers who must also have tired of her unending advances

Does Your Meter Work?!

A fifteen minute walk from Pham Ngu Lao Street is District 1, or typically known to the Vietnamese as "Saigon," where the class of hotels, restaurants, and bars are a notch higher and the prices at least double. Big, loud, steamy Apocalypse Now is the hooker hub. The bar scene is typical where each sex trolls, and each sex is in competition, and the short and long-term pairs do their googily-eyes. The major difference is greater displays of male chauvinism because the women are the more desperate camp.

The Western men know that any Vietnamese woman who's in the bar is a rare bird because she has the courage to mingle with Caucasians. Also, she either speaks English well enough or she can live with her lost face if she can't, and she's lying to her family where she is out so late. Lightning has been known to strike, but if anywhere it's here the hookers and husband-hunters mingle: the line is too fine to ever be sure who's who.

At night, walking means bids from roving motorcycle hookers. Mr. Glenn, my Canadian pal, had no patience and was nothing less than cruel in his brush-offs. At first, I humored the girls' requests but after some time, Vietnam's MANY angles of exploitation tired me. Loaded with pathology, I began stealing rides in a futile attempt to fight back.

"Where you go? You want massage?" she would ask.

"Let's go!" I'd call out, jumping on the back.

She was thrilled at such an easy close. Vroom, down the street.

"Go straight...now turn right...keep going...stop, STOP!"

Her head spun looking for the hotel as I walked towards my next destination.

"Thanks...see ya."

"No massage?"

"Nope, thanks for the ride."

"Money? Money?"

"Nah, no money."

Another wouldn't heed my directions and steered away from Pham Ngu Lao Street. I reached in front, removed the key, we coasted to a stop, I hopped off, and returned the key.

"Massage? Here? Where?"

"No thanks, no massage."

"Money? Money?"

"No, you wouldn't go where I asked, now I have to walk, no money."

She drove off.

Le Duan Street runs in front of the former U.S. Embassy. Vendors sell cigarettes by the one's and two's or, if you're sufficiently capitalized, the whole 20 pack for just over a dollar. Soup ladies teeter-totter poles across their shoulders, soup simmering on one end, and bowls, spoons, chopsticks, and garnishes balancing out the other. A zillion bicycles and motorcycles zoom about. The woefully underpaid venal police cruise in shiny new Jeeps and SUV's. The street girls line up at 20 yard intervals as if they're all waiting for the same bus.

Any ride on a three-wheel cyclo after 9 p.m. automatically detours down Nguyen Du Street, and takes twice as long because of the hoards offering flesh on foot. Broken streetlights outnumber the functional lights providing quasi discretion.

Lines of guys in shorts, dirty t-shirts, and flipflops lean palms first against a concrete wall or a closed store front's pillar like they're getting frisked, but the "lady cops" hands are checking furiously up and down for contraband in only one spot – front and center. Cockroaches big enough to burn diesel fuel scatter *everywhere*.

One afternoon, in my hotel, the front deskman knocked on my door.

"You have visitor."

"Send them up," I said.

"I can't."

"Why not?"

"She a lady."

"So."

"She a Vietnamese lady."

"So."

"It's impossible."

"Why not?"

"Impossible, can't do it."

He ran back down the stairs. Infuriated, I followed. At that time, I was working as an English teacher and my visitor was a student looking for help.

`NO VIETNAMESE FEMALE MAY ACCOMPANY A FOREIGN MALE TO HIS ROOM UNLESS THEY PRODUCE A MARRIAGE LICENCE' rang another rule from the posted boilerplate. The official excuse was it combated prostitution.

"Can a foreign lady go with a foreign man?"

"No problem."

"Can a Vietnamese man go with a foreign lady?"

"No problem."

"Can a Vietnamese man join a foreign man?"

"No problem."

"What if the Vietnamese man is a man prostitute or the two men are boyfriends and they have homosexual sex?"

Blank stares, closed lips, and emergency paperwork.

"So, a foreigner man cannot have sex with a Vietnamese girl but a foreigner man can have sex with a Vietnamese man in your hotel?"

"Two men no have sex!"

"Men don't have sex together?"

"No in Vietnam!"

The "mini-hotels", real hookers, and cops are in cahoots with payoffs. Even Vietnamese heterosexual couples rent rooms by the hour with only their ID cards, no marriage license.

Lead headline one week in The Vietnam News, the state-run English language newspaper: PROSTITUTION ELIMINATED IN HO CHI MINH CITY.

And then there's Hand Job Park…

HAND JOB PARK

Each day spent in present day Vietnam includes the following conversation from a cyclo driver:

You...YOU...MAN...where you go? You want cyclo?
No. Go away.
You. YOU! Massage? Fucky? I take you? Where you go?

Cyclo drivers know what men want; they just lack a little diplomacy. However, native Vietnamese men generally don't have the money for the full service, so they have their own place to park.

Now, back up in history.

During the 19th and 20th centuries, the French took a crack at their own little empire, for the most part failing, but they still managed to leave behind a few reminders of their sojourns into Indochina.

Two magnificent keepsakes, a Catholic Cathedral and the Post Office styled in grandiose Old European flavor stand out in the center of Saigon. Behind the Cathedral is a green area two blocks square.

Back to today.

You'll find leafy old trees, weedy grass that always needs cutting, iron benches, and vendors who sell snacks, smokes and postcards during the day. Next time you see that old footage on History Channel of North Vietnamese tanks crashing through the gates of the palace, and soldiers erecting a flag to signify the fall of Saigon, look behind the smiling victors and you'll see the park.

Beginning early evening after sundown, you'll find ladies sitting by themselves scattered about the park benches. Soon, a horny toad joins one, pulls down his pants, puts an arm around her to get real close, and she leans over. Any further movements come from the girl's arms. Facing the park with their backs to the street is their attempt at discretion. I sat waiting one night for a friend to never arrive and, upon my eyes from across the two-lane street, in less than an hour, a girl pulled four tricks.

Does Your Meter Work?!

During each trick, pedestrians passed by at a consistent canter, others slowed to a crawl for a quick peek-a-boo over a shoulder, then carried on leaving the pseudo-lovers to carry on.

The first three clients didn't last long. No sooner were they done, the girl jumped to her feet and walked to another bench with her tote bag over her shoulder and tissue paper wiping and cleaning her hand...you do the math. The men bolted equally quickly, fastening their britches as they went.

Not atypically, rain exploded with the usual marble-sized droplets. While everyone scrambled for shelter in restaurants and beneath the overhang of buildings, our little enterpriser whipped out her fluorescent yellow rain poncho and remained open for business. A young man bicycled up, peered inside her tightly drawn hood, spoke a few words, then they assumed the position. The giggling audience of vendors, women, children, and whoever found themselves staying dry, loved it.

Her little shoulders went up and down and up and down - he wouldn't pop. Twice, like a boxer sitting in her corner between rounds she stopped, then her bell would ring and she'd be back into the business at hand. Finally he relented and they were none too happy to move on in their respective directions, soaked to the bone. The guard who I'd made friends with over the weeks reported fees for services rendered in Hand Job Park at 5000 Vietnamese *dong* ($1USD = 12,500VND).

$TOLEN MONEY, OR A STORY MAID IN VIETNAM

I was in Saigon working as an English teacher. The pay was good and the hours plentiful, consequently I was able to save a few dollars. Stowing this money downstairs at the desk with all that foot traffic left me uneasy and, because I was a long-term guest, I never thought in a million years anyone would steal from my room. This naiveté would prove expensive. Within my clothes in a bureau, I'd hidden an envelope containing 3,500,000 Vietnamese dong, about $300. Another half million of petty cash lay on top.

One afternoon, I awoke from a nap to find a nasty windstorm had blown dust and dirt throughout my room. A double row of ventilation holes, each about the size of a brick, ran along the top of the wall. They obviously hadn't been cleaned for years.

On my way out to school, I inquired at the front desk whether someone could dust my room and arrange for these openings to be cleaned. The usual smiles and confirmations met my query. I returned about 9:45 p.m. to find the envelope missing and the loose notes left inexplicably behind.

First and foremost, I stipulate that it was my own fault for not securing the money downstairs where, apparently, someone was supposed to be responsible for it. Within my room, it was open season.

Spitting nails, I met Glenn, another Canadian who rented a room on the same floor, and infuriated him with my story. He'd already been ripped off three times and found it impossible for anyone to care. We spent the evening drinking beer, watching the faces of likely suspects, and scheming towards any plan to halt future infractions.

The next day, I informed the management and demanded my money be returned forthwith or faster. Serious cranium clay concealment at a new Asian Summer Games record greeted these commands. The manager correctly referred back to the posted tobacco-stained hotel boilerplate on the plaster wall:

"Not responsible for articles left in the room."

I was furious. The thief had to be a member of the hotel staff. Perhaps two rats working together, one as lookout, the other doing the dirty work. The likeliest candidate was the maid. Only she had liberty, and cause, to enter the rooms. My vent-cleaning request provided the perfect opening. The door remained open during her normal day-to-day cleaning, but she must have shut it to access the vents. Ergo her opportunity.

Three hundred United States dollars: It was equal to six months salary, grinding it out washing and cleaning.

I couldn't deny my blunder. To collar the chronic culprit, it was up to me, Captain Canuck. I stopped ranting and devised a plan.

I tore strips of newspaper the same width as Vietnamese currency and filled an envelope identical to the missing one. From a bar I took a pool cue chalk, the blue kind that smudges and stains. Using some tweezers, I scraped and scraped until collecting a plentiful amount of fine powder. I then filled the envelope and put the trap in the same spot as the stolen one. Anxiously, I came home after class each night and checked the decoy. Sure enough, three weeks later, the villain had bitten. The envelope was gone but not much of the blue powder was immediately visible. Scratching my skull, I spotted a few traces and splotches but not the amount I had expected considering the amount of dye in the envelope.

I had placed the lure on the third level of a four-level bureau. I turned over my black nylon day-bag lying on the floor directly below to find all the blue had spilled out, making a colorful mess.

To my advantage, however, the culprit had turned the bag over and cleaned the immediate area. Who else had the means to clean up such a mess other than a cleaning lady with mops and rags?

I speculated she was at home, apprehensive about coming into work the next day. If I didn't hit the roof and all stayed quiet on the Western front, she might think I hadn't noticed. She would enter my room while I was at morning class, look for more blue, and clean the remaining not-immediately-noticeable splotches within the bureau. She would have no purpose to clean these seemingly insignificant blue spots unless they were significant to her.

I took pictures to compare pre-morning against the (fingers crossed) post-morning crime scene and remained silent, stewing in my anger and plotting vengeance.

Does Your Meter Work?!

On the way to school the next morning, I dropped the film at a 1-hour photo place and picked up the pictures after class. Straight-faced, I went upstairs, but she hadn't cleaned the lingering evidence. Nevertheless, pow-wowing in my room with the daygirl, manager, and cleaning lady, they looked at me as if I were daft while I recounted the whole process. The evidence was just shy of a smoking gun but even their weak denials revealed their belief it could only be the maid, who, incidentally, remained as cool, and cold, as ice.

"You will agree it had to be someone from the staff, won't you?"

The manager nearly nodded when cross-examined under my seething duress. If I could at least wrangle a concession that a staff member was involved then I win some leverage towards the argument of restitution of the cash.

With the manager's endorsement, I went to the police. The drivers and vendors who hung about the neighborhood skittered like chickens when I pulled up on the back of a police motorcycle. The lawman (snicker) came to the room and the daygirl proudly walked him through the proceedings like she'd been part of the chase. Smiling, he looked at me as if I were daft, and returned to the precinct, leaving instructions for the maid to come down for questioning.

Nothing happened. A few days later, with no news forthcoming, I went to the cop-shop and located the policeman.

"Did you talk to the maid?" I asked.

"Yes."

"What did she say?"

"She say she no take you money."

"And...?"

He walked away. I could imagine their conversation.

"Did you take the money?"

"No."

"OK, you can go."

What I hoped for, but never got the chance, was to cater to his guaranteed venality. I conspired to privately reward him 500,000 if he retrieved my 3,500,000 VND. Half a million dong is around a month's salary for a member of Saigon's finest. (A policeman's official salary is +/- $40/month yet they drive expensive vehicles and live well. Connect the dots.) Assuming he retrieved the money, he probably would have denied all and kept it anyway.

With a drooped lower lip, I shuffled home, aware of the hopeless cause I was flogging, but still felt a burning desire for some sort of justice.

So, I rethought my course of action. Stage one, no more rent.

The first Thursday went by without a word. Then another, then another. I was three weeks behind before the day girl, Phuong (pronounced "Fung" with a rising intonation) braved anything.

"Mr.Jim, could you please pay for your room?" she asked hesitantly.

"I paid already," I countered, sweeping by the desk and snagging the key.

"Who you pay?"

"The night guy, whatever his name is."

"Noooooooooooooo!" her protesting voice trailing off as I climbed the stairs.

Later that night, the night guy, whatever his name was, took a crack at it himself.

"You can't have your key until you pay your rent," he defiantly trumpeted.

"I paid it already...to the day girl, whatever her name is."

"No you didn't!"

"Yes, I did!"

"Then show me the receipt."

"It's up in my room."

"Show it to me."

"I can't get in unless you give me the key," I said lunging for it.

"No, you didn't pay," he answered, avoiding my play.

"Give me the key or you'll see more than the receipt."

I walked around the back of the desk and plucked the key from his gutless grip.

"Next time you try that, my hand might slip and end up right here," I warned, pointing to his chin.

"OK fine, but you don't pay, I keep your camera."

Does Your Meter Work?!

His face beamed. I never had the illusion of getting away with anything. There was a point to be made. That point still eludes me but I couldn't stomach going quietly into the night.

The next morning was Saturday. As I left, Phuong was livid.

"You MUST pay your rent!"

"I paid it already."

"NO YOU DIDN'T!"

"Yes I did!"

"Show me your receipt."

"It's upstairs in my room."

"GO GET IT!"

"Come with me."

I wanted her to witness me looking in the same place the money went missing from, then throw my hands in the air, shrug, and sigh, "It's gone...someone must have stolen it."

She wouldn't bite. "No, go now, I no come up with you!"

I walked up halfway, paused a moment, then skipped back down.

"I'm sorry," I began, "but it seems my receipt is gone. I think someone STOLE it!"

"No they didn't, you MUST pay your rent or you cannot have your camera and passport back."

We had a meeting with the manager in the hotel office.

"You MUST pay your rent."

"You think I have your money, don't you?"

"YES, you MUST pay your rent."

"And you want your money, right?"

"YES, you MUST pay your rent!" Phuong was pounding the air now.

The manager piped in, "If guest no pay, the desk people's salary pay."

This was new, serendipitous data. It produced a shy, embarrassed smile from Phuong.

"Well, now: How do you feel when you know someone has your money, you know it's your money, and you can't have it even though you know where it is and who has it?"

Phuong looked at the manager, translated, and they both broke out laughing, nodding.

"You must pay your rent."

"I will when I get my money back," I balked.

"We don't know who have you money," they returned.

"Yes you do know who has it..."

"The maid say she no take the money. Nothing we can do."

"OK, I want the maid fired," smashing hard to the baseline.

"We can't do that," they easily volleyed back.

I knew this. Then the manager asked, "What do you want?" her body language suggesting, at last, yes, surrender.

I began my demands.

"I want my room cleaned everyday. Sometimes the maid doesn't come in the whole day, sometimes she cleans the room a little or not at all. I want you to use bleach in my room and Mr. Glenn's too, like you promised. I don't want to buy it anymore. I want to come home at night and not have the 'guard' scream that I'm waking him up. People have phoned me and left messages that I've never received. Or, they are completely wrong, same with Mr.Glenn. The messages come from Vietnamese who talk in Vietnamese and the boys on the desk shrug and don't care."

They became bored quickly, listening sardonically. Then I pulled out my trump card.

"And I want my vents cleaned."

This sat them up. At once did they enter into council through a staccato of racket. They paused.

"You mean, they no clean yet?"

"No, and I've asked for it, probably four times."

This wasn't a lie. With all the sound and fury of the original theft day, no one thought to inspect the vents. A couple days later, I had climbed onto the windowsill to find the maid had never touched them.

"When this all gets done, then I will happily pay my rent."

Vietnamese anger dissipates instantly. Like school children, we playfully shook hands with a newly found lightness and I left to see a private Japanese student. A sparkling room awaited my return, clean as a nun's mind, with colorful posters, a new calendar, and boasts from Phuong detailing how she and the maid scrubbed the room from beam to tile.

Satisfaction guaranteed.

Does Your Meter Work?!

But when I inspected the vents, the limitations to their surrender were clear: they still hadn't been touched.

Phuong's mouth hung open.

I placed a chair for her to stand upon and she looked into the vents for the first time.

"Oh, I see," she sighed.

"Was I wrong all this time?"

"No, you weren't wrong."

I sat on the bed watching a troika of cleaning staff arrive with tools and remove the mesh on the outer face of the vents. Pails, rags, soap, bleach, and the maid went up a bamboo ladder and her tiny, thieving arm scrubbed the little concrete tunnels. They finished the job without stealing or breaking anything, although they refused to reinstall the screen, and left footprints from spilled water out the door. I went downstairs and paid the bill. I was home again.

But the return was short-lived. My room shared a bathroom with another that was rarely rented. Two weeks later, I came home to find the room occupied, their door into the bathroom open, and bath objects everywhere. I taped a note to the mirror warning of thefts. A few days later, a knock arrived at my door. A young British woman thanked me for the advice, which she had failed to heed. Japanese yen and Thai baht equivalent to $450, stuffed deep inside her backpack, were gone. I liked my room and being near Mr. Glenn as we complemented each other so well, but repetition is a fine teacher. I relocated.

Thereafter, Mr. Glenn gave me a running account of the hotel staff's reactions. First, my love for the front desk girl was too strong. A few days later, their logic deteriorated to I left because Glenn didn't like the shorts I wore and I had even quit teaching at the school over it.

Glenn had lived there six months and always had problems but he liked his room too much to leave. They asked Glenn repeatedly why I left. His answer was consistent: abysmal service and treatment. They never seemed to believe him.

ORCHID

Hoi An, Chinese in influence, was a small, quiet, old town. Her pagodas, temples, and architecture -- not unlike Georgetown in Malaysia -- posed for many nice pictures during my day's pleasant meander through the time-honored streets. I felt like I "did" Hoi An enough for my purposes.

Mid-afternoon, with the sun beating down, my thoughts already on the way to the capital Hanoi, I ambled along a quiet residential street with some pleasing colonial French architecture. Outside one of the houses, a family had set up a standard Vietnamese version of a lemonade stand. An umbrella, a plastic table with matching stacking chairs, a few assorted candies, gum, smokes, Cokes, iced tea and they were in business. I walked past, got the usual "Sit down, please," from a fetching lass, I gave her the usual half-hearted smile -- this maintenance of diplomatic relations had grown utterly weary by now -- and continued on. A block or so later, the sightseeing ended and I turned back. I approached again and thought, "What the heck, let's have an iced tea, I've got nothing else to see. You never know what can happen." For some reason, I thought this lady, so easy on the eyes, could speak English. Soon it was apparent that she couldn't and I didn't care anyway. After a few moments, whom I hadn't noticed when she sat to my right, was her sister who could communicate on a decent level. We stumbled through a conversation, her eyes seething with hate for me as she reported how foreigners only wanted one thing and they were AIDS laden and the girls from the Vietnamese cities were bad. The sister was an angry young lady, 30, divorced with two young children, a vertical scar rising from the left corner of her mouth from her ex-hubby's beatings.

But there was something too interesting about her, including her name; Lan, which rhymes with Dan, and means *orchid* in Vietnamese. Her words, although broken English, recurrently conveyed more depth than the usual shallow, simple banter. As we talked, the noticeable hostility occasionally relented and a shockingly beautiful face surfaced. She wore long black hair past her thin waist. Deep, devouring, ebony eyes balleted above high cheekbones. A perfect jaw outlined a sultry mouth, and a turned-up button, the smallest nose in the history of Faceland. She was a fairy, dainty and petite, a little over five feet tall and under a hundred pounds, with everything in the right place. I couldn't take my eyes off her.

"Why you look me all the time?" she asked.

I don't imagine I answered.

Our conversation grew friendlier. With a devastating smile, she offered a hair wash plus massage at her sister-in-law's shop in the market.

"What kind of massage?" I asked.

"Wash hair, then massage arms, head, back, leg, feet, shoulder...."

She trailed off. My mouth broke out a smile that brought one to hers. Then she finished off the menu.

"And that's all," followed by a giggle.

"How much is the massage of 'that's all'?"

"50,000."

Four and a half bucks buying a change of scenery seemed like a bargain for my rippling male hormones. My eyes radared into hers.

"I'll get a hairwash and massage if you promise to give it to me."

Her dutiful "no" quickly reversed to "okay," but she first needed a switch of clothes. Walking together the few minutes to the nearby market, I noticed we gained the attention of the townsfolk examining, scrutinizing us. Out the corner of my eye, I saw Lan's gaze bolted straight ahead.

The sister-in-law's esthetics shop in the market was nothing more than a walled-off, bamboo-matted square among walled-off, bamboo-matted squares, and decorated with a few pails of water and a single bed with a thin foam mattress. A battered kerosene heater fired up to warm the water. I lay down, captivated but perplexed, my head resting on a somewhat soft vinyl-covered head-bench.

In Vietnam, massage means, ninety-nine and forty-four one hundredths percent of the time, prostitution. But Lan was no floozy and this was no whorehouse. She sat beside me. I didn't know what to expect.

"I do massage a little," she began, "But my sister, she much better. Better she do and no me."

The sister-in-law, who couldn't speak a word of English, nor could be considered at all attractive, began washing my hair, all the while Lan stayed next to me. I would come to find out that because of Lan's obvious endowments, both in language and looks, she'd drummed up business in the same manner more than once. I looked at her, the truth of her ruse now apparent, and we laughed together. I surrendered to the caper and enjoyed the effort of the sister-in-law's fingers. I slid my arm halfway around Lan's waist, which she did not resist, in spite of being in full view of anyone who may have walked by. An hour later, the pleasantries finished, I sat up. A drawn curtain separated us from the others.

At some point in the beginning of our contact, a tingle of unknown origin turned us into two conducting rods. A swirling synergy arced to combust a fuse, flaring in controlled fury for a source to detonate. Within our meager privacy, the immediate din of the market in the background, the dynamite blew when our lips touched.

Our faces severed.

Her bottom lip quivered. Her left eye twitched with dread. Her cast-in-stone traditional values always had a confused fear/hate of foreigners. What was she doing kissing this "philanderer" surrounded by the people to whom and where, everyday for the last 12 years, she had sold pork in this market? She was terrified, taken hostage by her zeal of the minutes. I wasn't doing any better.

"You know we like each other," I gasped, swallowing, "Kiss me again."

"I'm so afraid," she pleaded.

Our eyes were locked and loaded. I nodded. She trembled. I nodded again. She leaned forward and kissed me.

I wasn't sure how it all happened either, but at least I had an idea. I identified my own fervor thundering and surfed the wave. Western society allows more access to the powerful narcotic called passion. Fortuitously, I have a cherished friend of the female persuasion, an expert on passion's vitality, who had schooled me over the years. A platonic Mrs. Robinson, I had been able to run to her to sort out the turmoil that presently wracked Lan.

Does Your Meter Work?!

I pressed Lan to meet me later for dinner. A war raged within her trying to grasp the complex forces at work.

"I'm so afraid."

Distracted by the gossip from the other side of the curtain, she silently debated going further as we steadied ourselves. I backed off, giving her breathing space. My guts cheered her on. Her gears turned while she fidgeted with her hair band. She opened her mouth to speak. I leaned forward. Then her shoulders slumped in renewed contemplation. And then...

"Okay, I meet you but no until after like this," she agreed, pointing to a black portion of her paisley hair band. Teaching in Asia had taught me to interpret her meaning: after dark.

"Oh, thank you," I thought, then asked, "What time?"

More thinking.

"Seven o'clock."

"Where do I meet you?"

More thinking.

"My house."

"Your house, seven o'clock?"

"Yeah, and no like this," she said with resolve, lightly tugging on the leg of my shorts. "You take long pants, OK? Short pants, no good."

That was all I needed to know. Any more questions gave her the chance to rethink. I slid open the curtain to see three new girls sitting a few feet away on another bed, heckling and cackling like crows on a fence. Lan remained behind, I said "bye for now," then headed straight for my hotel.

Any quick pace opened perspiration floodgates. I entered my hotel lobby, only minutes away from the market, dripping. A bus full of tourists, just like me the previous afternoon, milled about the room, asking prices, deciding whether to stay, filling in reservation cards, and in my way. I waited impatiently to ask for my key, kind of hopping on one foot like a little kid needing the bathroom. Everyone took so long tying up the desk clerks. I sliced closer to the front of the quasi-queue, one of the girls recognized me as an already registered guest, and fished her hand by two people with my room key. With self-imposed leniency to manners, I overrode her conversation with another foreigner.

"I'm not leaving tomorrow morning."

"Oh? You stay tomorrow?"

"Yes, can I keep my room?"

"Yes, no problem," she said, craning her neck, "How many days?"

"Indefinitely."

"Ind...huh?"

"More days, I don't know how many."

"Thank you, sir."

"Oh no, thank you Hoi An."

Big smile...rotten teeth.

After a shower, some pointless shifting of my things, and then laying down, I watched the ceiling fan spin, my mind blazing along three-thousand light years from home. The clock clicked 6:30 -- the home stretch in the frantic obsession of clock-watching. Now, there was no turning my back on seriously calculating precisely how many units of time before 7 I should leave, allowing for distance, rate of speed, length of stride, and how many minutes after 7 I should get there...perhaps I should show up early?

Tick. Tock. Time to leave.

Maybe I just shouldn't go, I could leave in the morning, she'll never know, after all, what are the chances she's going to go through with the evening? Four to one says she's not there, that her sister will say, "Lan busy, Lan no here" and in reality Lan's hiding out in the back. Think of the times you were stood up in Saigon. Yeah, then it will be her that chickened out. After all, I showed up, right? What, are you crazy? Ah, you know, just being a coward. Money, don't forget that, I imagine I'm buying. I better stop at the desk for more, where's my key, what else should I take, my little flashlight? Nah, don't think so. Money's all. Check my teeth, no cilantro, good, did I shave close enough, it's tough, eh, with only a battery shaver and sweating so much. I should have used the foam and razor but then I might cut myself. Good decision, Jim, you got it together this evening. Whoa, is my fly up? OK, I'm outta here, just turn off these lights. Click. Where's the key? Lights please. Click. I don't see it, you didn't leave it in the bathroom, did you? Yeah, here on the sink, ya dumb shmuck. Click. Is the door locked, OOPS, where's the key? Ah, good, in my hand. Whew, it's hot in the hallway without circulation.

Does Your Meter Work?!

Down the steps to the desk. The lobby was graciously empty except for the desk girl, a new one just on shift.

"Good evening, sir."

"Good evening, could I have my pouches from the safe with my money, please?"

Is anyone as jaunty and spruce as I? Geez, how much more will I need? How much do I have in my pocket now? I counted it three times in the room and can't remember. Doesn't matter, I'll take another 300,000, that's gotta be enough. I better rewrap my pouches without fumbling lest the clerk watching so intently begins to think I'm nervous then she'll deduce I have a date and you know how the Vietnamese gossip, she'll tell everyone in the hotel, OH NO!, first I said I was leaving tomorrow then changed my mind, I'm sure she heard. Shit, I'm sweating already.

"Here's my things, and the key, thank you."

"Thank you, sir."

Big smile. Rotten teeth, too. Does she know <u>already</u>? I set out.

Are my pants all right? Oh, man, they're hot after only a couple steps, I'm gonna sweat like crazy, they look dumb with sandals and no socks but I got laughed at by my students in Saigon for wearing socks. This shirt, light cotton with a collar and rolled up long sleeves, white and teal vertical chalk lines, goes with the khaki pants but a brown belt and black sandals? What can you do, you're a traveler, it's not like you have a complete wardrobe to choose from. RELAX! Relax? That's easy for you to say. Of course it's easy for me to say, I'm you, ya dope. OK, I'm relaxed, but what will <u>she</u> wear? I hope she doesn't doll up cuz if she shows too much of that yummy little body, I'm gonna be intimidated as hell. Gawd, she's beautiful, it felt incredible when I put my arm around that miniature waist of hers this afternoon, pleez don't make yourself too beautiful, Lan, I won't handle it.

Nearing the house, my butterflies were in full jailbreak. I saw Lan squatting down, talking to a child seated in a chair. She looked and leaped straight up, blasting a waving hand into the air with a perfectly straight elbow. Her body language doused some fears -- and stroked my brittle ego.

Did you see that wave! Oh man, she looked happy to see you, as in me, you know what I mean. Whew, I feel better. I've never seen anyone so happy to see me before. I guess she doesn't know me too well yet. Maybe she should?!

She tugged shyly at the front of a sleeveless, one-piece mini-dress. Light bounced off too much deeply tanned, perfectly smooth skin for my insecurities, now running riot from their cage.

Oh no, look at her. Oh damn, if she wears that to dinner, I'm a goner...finished...kaput. Calm yourself, calm yourself. She looked shy pulling her dress down, didn't she, DIDN'T SHE? Trust your eyes, buddy, she sure did.

"*Xin chao* (pronounced sin-jiao, means 'hello')," she said, "Sit down, please."

Vibrating, I sat in a chair much snugger than earlier that afternoon. Its cheap plastic legs, pushed out by my Western mass, made a scraping sound on the sidewalk.

"I change clothes, you wait, OK?"

"You don't want to wear that?"

"Oh no, this for my house, not for go out there," she answered, waving her hand towards the horizon.

She disappeared into the house and reappeared wearing white silk pajamas with a rose pattern, buttoned to her neck, with long sleeves and the legs covering her feet.

"Whew," went more of my emotional instabilities as I stood up. The chair, wedged against my hips, followed me up, then popped off and fell to the ground as I straightened at the waist. The small crowd of kids and neighbors loved this one. We started walking.

"I like your new clothes," I said.

Only a smile.

"Are you shy to wear a dress?"

Bigger sheepish smile.

"So, you know where we should eat?"

"I don't know. You say."

"I don't know. You live here. Is there somewhere that you like to go?"

"I like to go restaurant have no foreigner."

"You are shy that foreigners will see us together?"

"Yeah."

"Me too, a little bit."

Does Your Meter Work?!

By now, we were nearing the restaurant closest to my hotel where I had had breakfast.

"Do you want this restaurant? I had breakfast here this morning."

"You say."

"Well, no, you say. I want to take you to anywhere you want, maybe a special place you like, or to somewhere you won't feel shy."

"She my friend," said Lan, pointing to the restaurant.

"Are you shy for your friend to see us together?"

"No her, I like."

"We can go there if you want."

"You say, I follow you."

"All right, then let's go farther down the street to another place where I had dinner last night. I know it was good."

Now we were even with her friend's restaurant.

"No, I want here," Lan confessed smiling, turning 90° and grabbing my arm, then letting it go just as quickly.

"I want here too."

At the table, it was magic. And so simple. I couldn't speak at first, only look. The restaurant owners, who knew Lan so well, constantly peeked up while preparing the food or from around corners. Because of our audience, officially Lan was supposed to be angry with my stares, but she couldn't do it.

A magical gas effusion, blown by the other person, is inhaled, casting an all-consuming analgesic spell of gladness, fantasy, calm, and harmony. You are supposed to belong together, like you've known them your whole life. Your entire history was training for the now, finally opening a passage to disclose all the things previously accomplished, thought, believed, felt, decided, and so forth. Ordinary, mundane events take on profound meaning. The pieces of the jigsaw puzzle seem to float down from the sky and fall effortlessly into place the way the universe ordained.

I had originally planned to leave the next day. I reconfirmed my room for three reasons: First, to cover my bases, second, I had nothing to lose, and third, panic. During dinner, when Lan said, "If you stay tomorrow, we can go the beach," I knew for sure the bus would have one empty seat. Afterwards, she led me to an ice cream parlor that set up in a school ground in the evenings. The spacing between the tables and the dark night permitted privacy. Romantic aftershocks from the earlier afternoon's earthquake resonated. Our single order of coconut ice cream was left as a puddle on the plate.

I knew I needed to be careful but the day had been too explosive to pretend it didn't happen. The look on her face and the sound of her voice dazzled me, not in an awe-struck, Hollywood sense, but in a sincere, absorbing, "for real" package. Providence used the day to pose possibilities that demanded and deserved to be explored with a free and exposed heart. I vowed to use the time remaining on my visa to jump into the deep end and do the experiment. I wanted to add my half to our whole without holding back. For her sake, my spoken words would be straightforward, candid indicators of how I felt. For my sake, the intention behind the words would be uttered bearing a full disclosure of my heart. To let go of this situation flippantly would lead to personal regrets. Old, traditional beliefs and the threat that I could exit at any time left her vulnerable to twisting in the wind. Her home-field advantage exposed my flank. Either of us could use these vulnerabilities as a stick on the other. I had no intention, nor any fears of her.

For the next ten days, Vietnam was seen through rose-colored glass like Bergman and Bogey in Paris. Lan finished her work by 11 a.m. We went to the beach, took pictures, drove through the countryside on a rented motorcycle, shared meals. Her upbringing, conditioning, traditional societal norms told her she was wrong, bad, dirty.

"Why, why, I am with you?" she begged rhetorically, "never...I never wanted to know foreigner. Why, WHY I love you?"

I loved her too. The human frame possesses an obsessing, powerful, psychosis-inducing amphetamine called passion. In simple terms, you're finished. Enjoy the ride.

Speaking of rides, one day we hired a boat. The old, weathered lady who paddled us up and down the river in her flat-bottomed canoe changed her story at the end and wanted 20,000 VND per person instead of the previously agreed 20,000 total. There was an enormous argument, of course, in the middle of the market and I was laughingly shooed away while Lan took care of the negotiations.

Arguments Vietnamese style are basically a war of attrition. Screaming begins which draws a circular gallery. Whoever outshouts whom, a combination of decibels and endurance, wins. She underestimated Lan, assuming Lan would take the home side against the rich foreigner.

During our river cruise, we made pit stops along the empty banks. My camera, loaded with a fresh roll of 36 exposures, thoroughly enjoyed its job. With no one to snoop on us, Lan smiled and posed.

Later, at the development shop, all the photos turned out with typically some poses better than others. I opined that seven were keepers, and three of these rated as award-winners. Lan, however, was livid. She grabbed at each picture, filling her disgust reservoir more and more until it overflowed.

"The pictures, very ugly, I don't like!" she ranted.

"They look good to me..."

"NO! Why you take ugly pictures of me, no beautiful, WHY?!"

"But they are nice pictures of you, look, you're smiling, you have your Vietnamese hat on, not all of them are wonderful, but probably six or seven are OK. And look at these three, I like these three, they're very beautiful...."

"NO!"

Lan vented to the supportive clerk who nodded agreeingly, and shook her head, complete with "tsk, tsk." A picture in Asia should portray timelessness, steeped in tradition, to last for eternity. The Western eye likes to catch an instant in time, to record what happened at that moment.

Lan went home seething, barely able to make the plans to meet at 7 o'clock. I returned to my room undecidedly -- sad for not pleasing her, slightly insulted because the pictures weren't awful, and inert of feeling as I knew nothing could change her mind.

That evening, I crept on eggshells to Lan's house. She laughed and smiled, happy to see me, all was forgiven, yet still not crazy about the day's events. She did relinquish two of the pictures at my insistence, but the chance of the negatives reaching my hands had as much chance as our coconut ice cream against the tropical heat.

Lan, her sister Xi (pronounced see), and I tripled on a motorbike 10 miles to spend a day at the beach. Two foreign women sunbathed nearby who, to my Western eyes, were not in the least bit appealing and probably wouldn't be considered so by many others. Rather overweight and of pale complexion, these whales-on-the-beach would have to work hard on the Personality and Interests section of their "For Singles Only" ad.

My companions, hiding under the shade of big beach umbrellas, couldn't understand why these girls laid in the blazing sun. Lan -- with dark skin, even for a Vietnamese -- and Xi agreed that Lan's skin was no good. Traditional Asian theory dictates that poor people have dark skin from working all day in the fields. Skin stays white by spending time in the house, too well off to be outside working. In the West, tanned skin shows enough wealth to afford expensive holidays under the sun. Anyway, my ladies envied the coloring of these "beauties" and concurred that their largesse made them look strong and well fed.

Anyone of African descent has little chance in Asia. I had been acquainted with a few African-Americans who had come to Taiwan to work. Well-educated and well spoken, they left after only a few weeks, the handwriting clearly written on the wall. Their black skin, thought to be too repulsive, made it impossible to get hired.

Five dollars rented a 100 c.c. motorcycle and the two of us spent a different day at deserted Hami Beach, an hour plus away. Going home, Lan rode side-saddle, snuggled close, her slender left arm enveloped around my chest while her right hand tried straightening the curls on the back of my head. Resting her chin on my shoulder, she sang Vietnamese ballads in my right ear. Then it was my turn to croon. All I could come up with was a brutal rendition of Come Together. Thankfully, she didn't ask for an English clarification of "Here come ol' flattop/he come groovin' up slowly." It also wouldn't have been unreasonable on her part to inquire the English meaning of Shoomp do doodle dooooooooo doo, the bass guitar plucks I volunteered at no extra cost, but she was just happy I would sing for her. At any rate, the noise of the engine drowned out any chance of discriminating any lyrics as my serenades floated off into the rural night sky.

Does Your Meter Work?!

At night, cockroaches and rats perambulated in and out of her house, a concrete square about the size of a big master bedroom. Late in the war, North Vietnamese Army soldiers had stormed the house looking for Lan's paratrooper father. They found him lying in bed with a broken back and miraculously spared his life. Now, he hunches about, his thoracic vertebrae mangled and protruding.

Out behind the house, an addition of bamboo poles lashed together held up a crude roof. The bathroom had a cold, concrete squat toilet with no light. The family cooked using a wood fire and lowered a bucket into a well for water. I wondered if Lan ever had slept on a mattress, sat on a toilet and idled through a magazine, or felt the soothing sensation of a warm shower.

A couple of times, after everyone was asleep, while we were busy playing tonsil hockey in what would have been the living room, rats chirped and scurried along the walls, under the furniture, and up to our feet to investigate.

Our conversations were intense and riveting. English was the only choice available. Through osmosis, my Vietnamese had grown to *hello, how are you, I don't know, I don't understand, you're a big liar, excuse me, why, thank you, very beautiful, sorry, where are you going, iced tea, iced coffee, you're crazy, no MSG, two bottles, very cold, no money,* and last but not least, *orchid.*

Lan was reluctant to speak because of, card one, her innate Oriental reticence, card two, limited abilities in the language, and card three, the wild card, *losing face* anytime she couldn't understand or communicate -- a serious, personal crisis on Lan's side of the wall. Losing face can arise at anytime, under any circumstances, and be thoroughly disguised. Under siege by our hormones, discombobulated blood chemistries contributed to distract me and, I'm assuming, added extra pressure on Lan to not screw up from her point of view.

By acclamation, I was elected spokesperson because, card four, I could, and card five, I wanted to. I wanted to show her the way, that by talking about my feelings vicariously gave her permission to talk about hers, and demonstrating that death does not arrive unto the doorstep of someone who shares these "corrupt" thoughts.

Does Your Meter Work?!

Limited language ranges meant it was crucial to hang onto and milk each utterance, as every syllable carried a poignant urgency. One of us would go into an extended monologue and the other would hold on to each breath for dear life. Sometimes, after a long speech and careful concentration, the meaning was impossible to grasp and an "I didn't understand" would burst the balloon. Mistakes and misunderstandings became a "share." Each new word was something we did together, unusual because she remembered the words.

Lan asked me to come over at four one afternoon for English lessons. Her son sat in a little chair at a little table printing Vietnamese letters. Lan and her daughter sat at the big table, the little girl writing a story, in Vietnamese, and Lan copying English words on a damaged blackboard -- old and beat-up enough to have been used on The Mayflower. The butts of chalk powdered onto the floor as she wrote. I corrected spelling mistakes until she protested, "My this say no." According to her "this," an English/Vietnamese dictionary, I had spelled the word incorrectly. Her eye was right but the dictionary was wrong. I thumbed through the tattered, yellow-paged book and found all sorts of mistakes. I confiscated it and spent the next day digging up an Oxford English/Vietnamese and English/English dictionary. Her smile of gratitude was as wide as mine of validation.

Lan was too shy to sit at a sidewalk table among the foreigners, but on this evening, she was brave. In the middle of a romantic googly-eyed dinner, a flying cockroach the length of my pinky crashed into my forehead and landed in my bowl of soup. I sprang out of the chair like a Bouncing Betty landmine, the full force of the other English patrons' laughter ringing in my ears from the unforeseen dinner show. It absolutely grossed me out to witness the trespasser do the Front Crawl amidst the broth then regain its senses to begin enjoying the fare. Lan found it and me rather amusing, her chin resting on her folded arms on the table studying the dinner intruder and wondering what the word for this thing was in English.

The waiter brought new soup, we resumed googly-eyes, and the pest's twin brother bounced off my left cheek into my fresh bowl.

"Cockroach!" declared the gold-star student.

Does Your Meter Work?!

One evening, the conversation came around to fear and being afraid. I asked if "we" scared her.

"I'm afraid you go far from Hoi An, go other countries, go your country, stay in Canada, then come in Vietnam and come in Hoi An to visit me. Maybe I no here, maybe I marry someone and go far from Hoi An. You come to visit and I no here and you are sad...and me too."

"But if you marry someone else, then you will be very happy, no?"

"No," she hushed, her eyes dropping to inspect the hem on her blouse. "No."

What if I stayed longer? What if I opened a business here? Hoi An could use a bar catering to à la carte travelers. It would be cleaner than anything else around, that's for sure, the bathrooms would be modern. How would the other business people react? Would I be accepted into the fraternity or ganged-up on as an outsider, a too-rich, privileged foreigner who doesn't rate co-operation and help? If the lady in the boat was any indication, they would surely try to drive wedges between Lan and me. Would Lan or her family receive fall-out from the neighbors? Would her family have unrealistic expectations of Lan brought about by our association? Would hard feelings be laid on my doorstep or on Lan's? Can I burden her with problems caused by my own Canadian needs? Staying would mean ditching my culture, my family, friends. Someone has to give up almost entirely what is comfortable for them and that's one hell of a sacrifice; a sacrifice commanding such special attention above and beyond what is reasonable to ask of a spouse. These issues don't go away, Jim, think about all of them. What's on Lan's mind? I wish I could know everything. All these issues don't detract from the situation's magnificence but still are omnipresent, always churning.

Lan's lone experience with the opposite sex was becoming a teen-age bride with her first and only boyfriend. Marriage is a business deal. One is not "complete" unless married and in the family way. "Nice" girls do not play the field. Lan's typical role was to bear children and satisfy him when he came home drunk and horny. The enormous pressure on women -- including violence -- to produce sons has eased. Ironically, the male, with his XY chromosome, is responsible for the selection of the offspring's sex.

Does Your Meter Work?!

I raised my glass of iced tea as a toast. Lan raised her glass, the top edge clinking halfway down my glass. She explained that in Vietnam, the woman touches her husband's glass at a lower level. I lowered my glass, flush with hers, in symbolic disagreement. She dropped hers in symbolic "sticking to the tradition." We lowered and counter-lowered until both glasses sat on the tabletop. I slid mine over and clinked them. She smiled in appreciation at the gesture but still didn't like it.

What if we stayed together for a long time? A bizarre competition could spawn as I tried to give her more equality than she was accustomed to, as she struggled to adjust to a situation that was closer to a 50-50 partnership.

The reasons behind my being beyond my 20's and still single were opaque to Lan. In fact, many times while in Vietnam, I wasn't believed that no one back in Canada waited with my name on her.

"If I had a wife back home, I would be there with her, not over here traveling in Asia," was my typical response, logical I felt, but nevertheless received with skepticism.

Lan needed to know about my previous girlfriends, Western society's relatively liberal freedoms a source of both envy and dislike. Ten years earlier, I had lived a three-year common-law relationship. A setback with Lan was that I didn't marry the woman during this time. I tried explaining that the reason was simple: neither of us wanted to - the pressures in my world were different than hers.

No sale.

I knew she wanted to dig deeper, asking more about the philosophical underpinnings of my/our "terrible" decision, but she couldn't. Rage prevented her from asking what she wanted. She only asked, "Why, WHY, you no marry her?"

Trying to handicap the true reason for her upset was an inexact science at best. The smart money said the threat of her losing face by not being able to communicate accurately held off added grilling. Another possibility was she is conditioned, during touchy subjects, to not hearing the truth. Any answer that wasn't immediately satisfactory automatically became a lie on my part. Lan was aghast that the lady and me invested three years -- and we were well into our twenties, for Pete's sake -- and I hadn't married her, like it was my sole responsibility to make the blessed day happen. Perhaps my dereliction of duty by not making an honest woman out of this previous love invaded Lan's allegiance to the female union. To further explain my position, I tried guessing what other questions she may have had, but couldn't ask. My attempts only multiplied her disgust. There was also no point in trying to change her mind.

Revealing my ownership of condoms was another setback. She had never seen one before and was rattled by finding it in my pocket. I didn't want to push too hard but, rolling the dice slightly, I didn't discourage her from finding it either. To her, condoms meant only AIDS and carrying them could only mean I already had AIDS. Condoms were only used to contain the disease within the offending body. I acknowledged that I carried condoms to avoid getting sick from another person whereas if I already had AIDS, then I would be back in Canada, under medical treatment, not traveling around the world.

I propositioned that if she were to become as agreeable as I to the notion of us to step into the lovemaking arena, then our purpose for condoms would be birth control. Her gears turned and I left that alone to stew.

Lan was well known in the small town from being the Belle of the Borough and a long time merchant. We walked together on the streets and were conspicuously noticeable. Me being six feet, with curly hair, and foreign; her being her. Her many friends' pointing and apparently good-natured teasing wrought glamorous smiles to her lips.

Lan limited her translations of others comments to, "They say 'beautiful couple'." Occasionally we would stop to talk, Lan getting grilled about this whopper she caught, and they would check me up and down like anglers spinning the story of landing a big one.

Not everyone was so magnanimous. A young teenager unabashedly circled us on his bicycle for blocks, staring like we were aliens. A faction of males would not accept seeing their women with others of another race. Their voices yapped biting, malicious tones. Mostly, Lan remained sober-faced and wouldn't translate, only saying, "No, no nice." One time, she did. For some reason, she found it funny this time. It took a few minutes to make herself understood, and laughing throughout the explanation, basically the insult was "That big, white dick will split a little girl like you in two."

Geez, what if I stayed longer? Would these hateful attitudes weaken, mitigated by my familiarity, or fan their flames of hatred and swirl into greater destruction? What will Lan face after I leave? How much ostracism awaited her? Was I setting her up for future grief? Will she be tainted, wearing a big scarlet A on her chest? Are my needs to be next to her selfish? I wish I could know but that damn cultural wall is too high to peek over. All I could do is follow her.

Locals continued to stare and my frustrations ignited. They would see us coming from down the street, their eyes locked in, their faces beginning sober, empty of expression.

As we approached, they would point and laugh, their crassness a one-way street. As a traveler, their hypocritical disrespect could be sloughed off but now, since I converted to a temporary resident, my sense of dignity demanded to be heard.

How can I protect Lan from these derisions? I must defend the honor of my fair maiden. I know, tomorrow, I'll buy a gun in the market and carry it loaded for a few evenings.

The next night, sure as Siberian snow, the stares continued. Clandestinely reaching into my pocket, with Lan slapping at my arm, saying, "Noooo, noooo," her warnings fell on deaf ears.

I'll show you jerk-offs to gawk. Yeah, that's it, keep lookin', keep lookin', just a little closer into range.

I aimed from the hip and twice pulled the trigger firmly. Revenge arrived! *Ffffffft!, Ffffffft!* Two beams of water jettisoned out of the night to pour cold water on their unmindful complacency. Lan laughed and laughed at my brash gall, hiding around corners to buckle over, slapping her knee, slapping mine, interrupted only by, "you cwazy" (she had difficulty with the "cr" sound).

The cat that lived at the restaurant where I usually ate rapidly learned that she and her fleas weren't welcome around my table. A few well-directed sprays from my weapon rammed the idea into her head to stay clear. The gun eventually backfired because of the unrestrained children. I squirted a few, my first mistake. Swiftly, a gaggle of rug-rats collected when I sat at my table, and then soon fought tooth-and-nail for possession of the gun. I was relieved when its high quality construction gave out after three days.

This simple beginning set off unimaginable repercussions within the community. Two nights later, sitting in the beauty shop, three of Lan's friends, acquaintances, associates -- I couldn't know what her relationship was with these people -- began roasting my character to Lan, while I sat next to her. They pointed, their faces angry, body language and voice tones saying that I was a dreadful person, inventing greater crimes than not letting their kids play with my gun. Lan sat motionless, listening, occasionally glancing over at me. Her expression divulged nothing. I didn't know if she now hated me from this diatribe of propaganda or if she wanted to slap my inquisitors. After they left, I asked what the hell went on. She was angry, appalled, I believed, at them.

She only said, "They say bad things, you no friendly, no nice."

Would she be swayed, automatically siding with their camp, or stick to her guns and make an independent decision based on her own gathered information about me and who I was to her?

"What do you think of what they say?" I asked.

"I don't care, they no good, I don't care."

With responsibilities catching up on Lan, my afternoons regrettably became free. I whittled away the hours trying to read, write, sleep, anything to avoid the midday sun and push the clock to move faster. With this time to meditate where our relationship had traveled, I wondered everyday if tonight would be D-Day where she would ask/tell/demand/require me to pack my bags and be out of Dodge before sunrise.

But she was always there, her complicity extraordinary. I felt like a fool for doubting her after the fact, but it was high tension until her smiles and wiggles of excitement let me off the hook. The majority of times it was me who brought up the point of formulating plans for the next meeting. I would ask about the next day and she put the ball back into my court by asking what I wanted. I tried to explain that there was no such thing as enough, I wanted to see her everyday -- all day -- but had to route the decision to the business of everyday life. She had work and children and family. I had only her. I couldn't help it, at the end of each evening, I feared the possibility she would tell me we had to be finished.

Why does she do this? Is she avoiding the topic? Is she shy, stuck in her feminine role? What's going on in her home, behind the closed doors of her family? Is she torn between pressure from home and her feelings for me? What about her children? Do they miss her, I can hear them asking, "Where's my mom? Where does she disappear to each evening, and sometimes for the entire day? She was always here before." What are Lan's parents talking about? She's never turned me down. Until she tells me different, I gotta take at face value that she wants me to stay. Everything must be kosher on her side of the wall...but what if it isn't? What if she's too afraid to tell me that I'm causing her big headaches? Her family seems very nice. Is she sacrificing herself for me?

I trusted she made her decisions for specific reasons although often they didn't immediately, if ever, manifest themselves. Maybe I couldn't understand but throughout I deferred to her territorial advantage and put any vulnerability I had into her guardianship.

Lan awoke every morning at four and rode her worn bicycle with no brakes and gripless tires out of town a couple miles to buy pork from a farmer. Then she prepared it to open for business at 7. She paid 16,000 VND per kilo and asked 22,000, not always getting it. She fed at least nine people: her parents, two sisters who each had one baby, Lan's kids, herself, then whoever happened to come along that day for a meal. To have ten siblings always meant guests. I asked Lan about her sister's husbands, or at least the fathers of their children. She looked straight into my eyes without a flinch nor an answer.

"You don't want to tell me?" I buckled.

"Why you ask me?"

Ooops.

She bought food everyday spending around 20,000 VND ($1.81) and tried to save 30,000 each day into the bank. Not everyday was a winner but she lived comfortably. Her kids went to school wearing reasonable clothes, she took them to the small amusement park, bought ice cream and souvenirs, and lived a middle-class English existence.

What would happen to Lan's family if I took her away? She's the sole supporter of all these people. Do I promise monthly alimony? Sister Xi could take over the business but the competitiveness of the market means customers buy from a specific person. Lan's departure would free her established customer base of 12 years to re-choose where they bought from. This puts the family's well-being and status quo into jeopardy. Vietnam being Vietnam doesn't permit a lot of second chances. Career changes are treacherous on their best day.

Lan's daughter, ten, was a sweet, lovable, quiet girl who did her homework and listened to her mother. Her son was right off a Norman Rockwell calendar. A black eye, scuffed knee, and a frog in his pocket, he was six years old and pure terror.

He took an instant affinity to me and I couldn't deny I was moved by it all. Vivid, torrid flashbacks of my childhood and of my father, who died when I was 14, overflowed the theater of my mind as I played with this little critter and heard him laugh with irrepressible trust.

As I waited for Lan, he crawled onto my lap, put his arms on my shoulders, and gently laid his head against my chest. This short encounter teased a cavernous vacuum in me and the truth was I wished it could have been much longer and frequent but the reality of the entire situation was no secret. Independent of both of our needs, we were being shortchanged. The difference in our citizenships was immutable.

Please don't do this because I may be forced to enjoy it thereby showing vulnerability, and furthermore, I'll give you exactly four hours to stop...and furthermore, furthermore, DON'T LET YOUR MOTHER SEE!" Ahhh, rats, she's looking out the window. "Hello, Mom."

One evening, while saying goodnight and formulating plans for the next day, Lan said she would be finished work later than usual. I asked how she knew. She pointed to the sky and said it was cloudy. My "hmm" with a rising intonation and scrunched eyes implied further explanation.

The clouds hid the moon. The fish couldn't get a bearing on their depth and would rise closer to the surface, enabling the fishermen to increase their harvests. The next day's market, flush with fish meant less demand for expensive pork. Under clear skies, the fish could see the moon, remain at a deeper level, and less fish strengthened Lan's prices. Few people had refrigeration so grocery shopping was a daily, even meal-to-meal, chore.

"So clouds are expensive," I remarked.

Not an easy statement to comprehend in a foreign language, she deliberated for a second, then laughed. Best of all her face presented a sense of accomplishment by understanding the innuendo.

Once per lunar month, a decoratively arranged offering of fruit on a big plate is set near the small temple that every house has. Flowers brighten the drabness. Taking turns, each worshipper vertically holds smoldering incense sticks with both hands at their foreheads and bows repeatedly while praying. Next, handfuls of rice are sown onto the street and phony money put to the flame, all in veneration to Buddha. Everything sits three days, then the fruit is eaten.

At dinner, Lan practiced chai (rhymes with "tie"; I don't know the proper spelling). Chai can last one, two, or three days, depending on the practitioner's devotion. They adhere to strict vegetarianism. No food may directly or indirectly contact meat. Of our shared rice and vegetables, Lan filled and refilled my bowl using her chopsticks, but not vice-versa, as my chopsticks had touched our standard fish and pork dishes of which all were mine for three evenings. Lan ordered tofu, extra vegetables, and more rice. She wouldn't drink from my iced tea glass nor allow our bowls to come near.

"So, tell me Lan," I asked, "Since my lips touched the fish and pork, does this mean your lips cannot touch mine for three days?"

Yikes, maybe I shouldn't have asked that. I'm only joking, and she's thinking about it but she obviously takes her Buddhism seriously. Oh good, she's got the meaning now and she's laughing. Whew, that could have been close. Whadda I know about the ins and outs of Buddhism, it seems so foreign to me but it's something she's deadly sincere about. Oooo man, if that one turned out to be an insult, I'd be in heap of trouble. Be careful, you jackass.

Does Your Meter Work?!

I would like to take this time to express my gratification towards the lack of restrictions imposed upon lips post-comestibles by not interfering in the smooching process.

We progressed at Lan's pace and slowly our contact grew increasingly carnal. One night, she led me through a maze of sandy jungle paths in the inky night presumably to visit her brother and his wife. We entered the yard through a gateless opening of a ramshackle fence, and I saw through the open door of the house a male passed out on the floor. Lan hustled me around the side of the house where the sister-in-law (not the massage sister-in-law) was rinsing the evening's dishes under a hand-drawn pump. They spoke a few words and the sister-in-law moved into the house where I heard her soft voice among her husband's groans.

"My brother drink wine tonight," Lan confessed, half embarrassed, half upset.

"This put the damper on our social evening," I concluded.

The bamboo house had two rooms with a concrete floor. The back room had a small clay extension for cooking that protruded out from one side with a crude chimney. Lan led me into the now vacated front room and we sat down on a bench. There was also a table and a bed with wooden slats covered by bamboo matting.

I waited for the sister-in-law to finish her chores then join us. Instead, she extinguished the light -- the only light -- in the back room and retired for the evening. Expecting to leave, I asked Lan about our hosts, was everything OK. Her simple nod indicated fine and she invited me to lie beside her on our own tumbledown bed in our own room.

The neighborhood grew quiet as time ate into the evening. In the jungle's humidity, the bright moon silhouetted palm trees through a window. Our rickety bed sounded cacophonous in the silence, the only near sounds were croaking frogs and, distantly, the odd barking dog. The bamboo matting itched. Lan's nightingale, accented, broken English whispers. Her long hair scattered feathering across my face, the odd strand tickling my mouth and tongue. Her hair smelled of orange from her sister-in-law's shop. The moving touches of her willowy, nubile body. Her skin smelled of Ivory soap, and felt like a cloud. The rose-petal touch of her fingers hydroplaned across my skin, each touch, each location, each timing, each raw instinct, impeccable. Two hearts can consummate their passion without necessarily including a mandatory orgasm in the conventional sense. All the biological toys raged as they were supposed to, linking the union of mind, body, and soul on our own terms.

Walking home, our bloodstreams swimming in natural opiates, I knew this was a watershed evening. Risking us together in the house pushed Lan to her outer limits, both as a person and a member of Vietnamese society. My foundations shook but with her entire reputation and esteem at stake, Lan must have blasted into a stratosphere she couldn't have previously imagined.

"Did you feel good tonight?" I asked like lovers do.

She grinned ashamedly and slapped my shoulder to leave her alone.

"No, no, come on. Tell me...did you feel good tonight...it's OK to tell me. I was there too and I felt very good. I'm not shy to tell you."

I watched, waiting for an answer. After a couple of gears turned, she nodded in a typical Asian way, thrusting her head in one quick, downward nod; not a painless confession for her.

"Oh, I knew it! Did you feel veeerrrryyyy good?"

"NO!" she spiked, not "no" to my question, but as in "no, cease and desist your questioning." She jumped up and down like a little girl throwing a tantrum, laughing out loud. The joy on her face was electrifying.

"I want you to tell me and not be shy...did you feel veeerrrryyyy good tonight?"

Two quick downward thrusting nods confirmed it. I stopped walking, put my hands on her shoulders, looked into her eyes, and asked,

"Did you feel wah - wah - wah?"

Lan buried her face into my chest. With a serious smile on my mug, I pulled her back and asked again.

"Did you feel wah - wah - wah?"

The streets were dead quiet. Under a light, her smile melted, her look deepened. I'd pushed enough. The decision to answer was up to her. Regardless, I knew she had experienced wah - wah - wah. I wanted to purge this bashful modesty and prove to her she could trust me. She did. A whispered "yes", she took my hand, and we walked in silence. A block of eternity later, Lan broke out in hysterics. Wah - wah - wah! Her heart translated this new word she hadn't come across in English class.

I knew from moment number one that being together in my hotel room wasn't ever going to happen under any circumstances, and immaterial to suggest so. It was illegal on Lan's part but, even more powerfully, immoral. We walked the remaining ten minutes to her house and began our good nights. Mother barked from the darkness to come inside. Lan walked me to the corner 30 steps away, kissed my cheek, and started for home. I stood and looked to see her turn to verify my departure. She twisted her face in mock anger, then smiled.

"Wah - wah - wah," she snickered and disappeared into the unlit house.

Lan's ex, of who she didn't like to speak, was out of her and her children's' lives. She left him, while pregnant, after he hit her with a thrown plate that caused the scar that rises above her lip.

She didn't whine about her tough life nor ask me for anything. She felt guilty about the wonderful meals and questioned why I always paid. Indeed, I was happy to fork out as the total damage hovered around $3.

I endlessly self-bargained as to how best to extend my stay. Hoi An was too small to have big English schools and teaching privately didn't seem like a feasible alternative.

Well, if I want to stay with her, the burden of responsibility is mine. If we stay joined, it's my call. I have the power and freedom to act. What if we went to Canada? Do I have the right to remove her children from their grandparents, aunts, uncles, and cousins? Would taking them away be better for the kids or a case of kidnapping? Who's better adjusted to assimilate into the other's community? Probably me.

In Canada, we'd have our own house. Lan would probably wonder where everyone is, why friends and family never seem to come over, why is home always so empty?

Another thing, she never worries about a baby-sitter. Kids in Asia blend into the crowd of people at their home. When her children become too much, she skips out to the beach or plays cards with her friends at the market without a second thought. Borderline abandonment by North American standards, Standard Operating Procedure around here. How would she react to feeling stuck?

What about staying in Hoi An and maintaining my sanity? The cultures are so different. Ohhh, I wish a satisfying answer that would work for both of us would just leap out and smash me in the face. We're in too deep if we do and heartbroken if we don't. Where's the compromise? And what's up with her not letting me watch her uncle beat up his kid the other evening when I picked her up, yet when I asked her about all the hitting and violence that goes on in Vietnam, before this night, she said it's necessary to make the children listen. How about when I drank all that water and then had to pee so bad. It was late and the streets were dark and empty, yet she wouldn't let me go on the street like everyone else, including her own son whom she didn't stop when we went to the amusement park together a couple nights ago. She made me hold it all the way to her house. Like a Navy SEAL, I inched by everyone sleeping to that bunker of a bathroom. I knocked over the plastic water scoop looking for a flush. Man, did it make a lot of noise in that silence. Was she just being on her best behavior, trying to be someone she's not? Could she adjust to living under Canadian habits? Does she really find this peeing anywhere and the beatings repulsive and I'm the vehicle for her to live the way she wishes but knows it's impossible? I give in to her logic, whatever that may be -- I'm too much of an outsider to understand. Besides, I simply don't want to upset her.

What about the standpoint of your own life, Jim? No one's calling you, needing you, they never have. To flick a switch and suddenly become a family of four hardly seems realistic. You can't stay in spite of compelling reasons to the contrary. If you weren't the luckiest person in the history of the world before meeting Lan, she has forever made your being a privilege to live. Her and Hoi An are not your Holy Grail, buddy. Your personal puzzle still needs pieces before the picture is recognizable and ready for mounting. Face the facts, friend, loving someone and what can be done about it are two separate issues.

Does Your Meter Work?!

Was the bi-polarity of Asia rearing its ugly head, preventing us from getting on with the business of living? Asia doesn't take care of people; it makes them scratch and claw, kicking and screaming for an everyday life.

Walking along during our final evening, immersed in chatter and play, block after block passed.

"Where are we going?" I asked, umpteen blocks later.

"I don't know...I just walk," she realized.

"Me too...I was following you."

"Oh...I follow you."

Lan chose to sit outside overlooking the river. A wine bottle covered in the melted wax from hundreds of burned candles centerpieced the table, reminding me of the gigantic tree roots swallowing the structures of Ta Prohm at Angkor Wat. We splashed on a huge, delicious, superb meal for $4.72. The decor included tablecloths and moist hand towels. I began to apologize for leaving.

"I know, I sad," she lamented, "I think my English make better, we can live together, and we are very happy..."

Her welled eyes welled mine. Putting down her chopsticks, she touched my face (without looking around to see who was watching), then took back the chopsticks into her hand,

"...but I know you have to go."

"I'm trying to write a book."

"Book? I don't know book."

"You know book." I mimed holding a book and flipping its pages.

"Ah, yeah, I know book...you make book?"

"I'm trying...during the day, when I wait for you, I write about us." I mimed writing.

She smiled lightly. Most people would have asked the gory details about what I wrote. Lan stripped our fish and filled my bowl.

Our parting sorrow held no sweetness. Cockiness borne from the freedom I savored turned to guilt by thoughts of leaving Lan behind. My saving grace was I knew her business would maintain her and her family. She teetered then finally agreed to my request to leave her $250 under the title of English lesson tuition. She feared the money insinuated vice.

Does Your Meter Work?!

Lan insisted I come by at 7 the next morning, a half hour before my bus departure. Stealing away from work to see me off, she wrote out her address, also a telephone number of someone down her street with a phone, then, if possible, please, "callaphone and story me." I gave her my address, but...I was a Dead Man Walking as we waited for the "all aboard."

I watched her canary Vietnamese silk pajamas fade away. She turned, we smiled -- hers stronger than mine -- and waved, but it was window dressing for all the gossips watching. The energies linking our conducting-rod hearts, stretched by the growing distance of imminent departure, dissipated and collapsed as she turned the corner. We had pressure-cooked an entire lifetime into 11 days. I imploded into my seat. She was pure and unpolluted. Grimacing, I left Hoi An for Hué.

ARE THINGS GOING POORLY IN NEPAL? NO SWEAT, THERE'S ALWAYS NEXT LIFE.

After a year of romping around South-East Asia, it became time to explore the Indian sub-continent. I hopped a plane in Bangkok, and replaced equatorial heat and humidity with the cooler, drier air of Nepal.

I arrived in Kathmandu without a guidebook, ergo no advance re-con for finding accommodation, meals, information, and so forth. Waiting in the immigration line-up, I borrowed another traveler's book for a moment to at least source the name of the tourist ghetto. The touts and shills know we are all rookies in their land but to not have *any* info would reveal unequivocally the gathered moisture behind my ears. *Thamel* was the place to be. At the exit door of the terminal, a man holding pictures of a room began his offerings:

"We have this room for you, sir, a very nice room."

"Uh-huh."

"It has a double bed, hot water, restaurant, everything..."

"How much is it?"

"We have many prices, sir..."

"I have about three bucks for a room."

"You can have a room for $25 or $18 and we have rooms for $6 available."

"You have rooms for $6?"

"Yessir, we do, and we have a car to drive you free, as well."

"What happens if no more rooms are available because, you know, sometimes the cheaper rooms suddenly are not empty when I arrive, or maybe, I don't like the room?"

"Then you pay the driver $2 for the taxi."

"Is the room in Thamel?"

"Yes sir, Thamel."

Nepal was supposed to be very cheap. Two dollars seemed a bit steep for the ride. With no way of knowing the distance from the airport, or the market rates for Nepal yet, I was susceptible to overcharging however, the arrangement didn't seem too pocked with loopholes and I felt in rush mode.

The little economy car twisted and hair-pin-turned around cows and between trees along a route no guidebook could be expected to detail. We pulled into a courtyard and up to the lobby. Inside, a well-dressed, clean-cut young man presented himself. He greeted me with a calm, rehearsed exterior.

"Do you have rooms," I began.

"Yessir, we have rooms."

"How much are they?"

"They are $25 for a single room and $45 for a deluxe double, sir."

"Well, there's only one of me and I want one of your rooms for $6."

"Sorry sir...all full."

"The man at the airport GUARANTEED you have rooms for six dollars!" I ejaculated, slapping my palm on the counter from lingering callousness picked up in South-East Asia. "You will give me a room for six dollars or I'm walking out of here and I won't pay for the taxi either."

The eavesdropping driver began a chatter in Nepali.

"Please, sir, have a seat, I must make a phone call."

In a few minutes, he returned and took a key from the board.

"Yessir, we have this room available. Please fill in this registration card and pay $6."

"I'll need to see the room first."

It had windows running the entire length, covered with curtains, rug on the floor, antique end tables on either side of a double bed complete with two thick quilts and really spongy pillows. There were reading lamps, countless electrical switches, and an antique desk with an embedded oblong mirror, perhaps used by Cinderella's stepmother. My still naïve image of Nepal said six bucks seemed exorbitant but the room was a masterpiece.

Kathmandu's elevation, just over 4000 feet, made a pleasant reprieve from the previous months enduring South-East Asian heat and humidity. The desk clerk had claimed the six dollars included hot water but only frosty poured from the tap, too crisp for comfort. An icy shower renewed the sensation of cold for the first time in a long while.

Does Your Meter Work?!

"I remember this," I thought, shivering as a breeze blew in through all those nice windows.

I dried off as quickly as possible and jumped under the blankets, pulling them tight around my neck, and exhaling through a little tunnel to trap warm breath and heat my body.

Nepal comes from the Sanskrit words *nipat alaya*. Ni, *down*. Pat, *to fly*. Alaya, *stay* or *house*. The references are to villages at the foot of the many mountains here. "A World Of Its Own" splashed the tourist posters and it certainly was no lie. Not wanting to be confused with India, Nepal Standard Time is rebelliously fifteen minutes behind, even though within the same longitude. Usefully placed between China and India, the Nepali government plays off these two giants, currying financial favors. Tourism ranks second in sources of income, only behind foreign aid. Average per capita income is a mere $200 per year, about the same as Vietnam and slightly ahead of Cambodia. Graffiti that says, "Vote for tree" with simply drawn trees competes with, "Vote for Sun" written beside rough yellow circles. The democratic party is "Tree," the communists "Sun." Illiteracy is so high, these basic, everyday symbols are campaign emblems for voters to know which party receives their ballot.

Kathmandu, a throwback in time, is an anachronistic platypus, (from Nepalese Kath = *wooden*, mandu = *temple*). Mostly gone now, 60's potheads and opium-indulgers congregated in "Freak Street." The commercialism has since moved to Thamel. Creaky mud and brick buildings with tiny alleyways that substitute for streets, just wide enough for two yaks to pass, are now trying to squeeze through 20th century vehicles. The old shops that must have once sported vegetables, carcasses, blacksmiths, goat's milk and who-knows-what else now dangle Chicago Bulls hats, Nikon cameras and accessories, and fluorescent Oakleys sunglasses. Tailors or seamstresses pedal away on manual Singer sewing machines in shops with unique styles, patterns, and colors of clothing and merchandise. There are tourist offices for trekking, shops renting equipment for the outdoor adventures, flights, buses, rafting, and moneychangers. Heaps of restaurants serve fabulous food at rock bottom prices in Greenwich Village type settings.

Does Your Meter Work?!

I was obviously in a different part of the world now. Hindu rather than Buddhist, mountains rather than jungle, dahl and dairy and potatoes rather than rice and fish and bamboo, clothing for warmth rather than to remain cool, the fleshy bodies larger boned and full-figured rather than slight and tight.

After a couple of days, Kathmandu, with all its sights and sounds, became too boisterous. My guidebook promised more tranquility in Pokhara, 120 miles away.

A rickety bus snaked along on a scrawny, well-worn, two-laned paved surface. The oncoming traffic, their journey uphill compared to ours, littered the roadside with outdated, under-maintained vehicles, which had overheated from the incline and dry, heated daytime air. Like ants to spilled honey, transport trucks gathered at accessible water spots from roadside streams to irrigate their steaming engines.

Nepal is too hilly for typical farming on extended flat plains. Unfathomable man-hours of backbreaking labor created acre upon acre of terraced farmland. Small streams tumbled down the steep mountainsides, channeled strategically to irrigate rice, wheat, and corn. It was early spring, the landscape brown, excitedly awaiting the coming monsoon to offer its gift of hydration.

The 120 miles took a spectacular eight hours. Pokhara (*pokhari* is Nepali for *lake*) is an idyllic little town of two parts. Schools, the post office, and all the businesses needed to sustain the critical mass occupy the commercial section. The other segment, *Lakeside*, is 15 minutes away by taxi. It's built along - duh - a lake, Lake Phewi that twists out of view around huge foothills, with the soaring, virgin white peaks of the Annapurna Range, and tallest mountains in the world, as a background canvas. Pokhara's only function is tourism with money laundering not out of the question. Guesthouse and restaurant construction feeds the economy, along with stores that feature clothes and souvenirs, also adventure travel shops.

I inquired at a guesthouse where a little girl with chestnut pigtails and a gap-toothed grin of sunshine smiled through the screen door. The landlord and lady were Andy, a transplanted Brooklynite, and his Nepali wife Mithu (pronounced Me Too). Hence their establishment's name *OM SWEET HOME, A NEPALESE-AMERICAN FAMILY JOINT ADVENTURE*. They lived on the first floor and rented five rooms on the second - 200 rupees per night ($1US = 60NR)

The next day was Andy's 50th birthday. His mother-in-law blessed him first by applying a mixture of flour, rice, water, and bright red dye to his forehead, then placed flowers behind his ears and in his hair. Red was Andy's correct color because he is a married man. Being a widow, she applied her own blessing of white. She finished by gracing the entire party with the red. Each shower, I tried washing around it, the belief being that the longer it stays on, the luckier the blessing.

Nepal is most famous for trekking. Five to six dollars a day rents all the gear. A guide is an additional $3 or $4. Most trekkers go for four to seven days, even up to weeks at a time. An expedition to *Sarangkot*, a hill station that overlooks Pokhara, exchanged shoe leather for a taxi most of the way and we walked another half hour to the summit. The mission was for an even more spectacular view of the Annapurna Range (anna is Sanskrit for food and pra is abundant. The fields at the foot of The Annapurnas were seen as a breadbasket), but cloud and rain washed out the idea. At least the room was cheap - 20 rupees (33 cents) - for a double, off season!

Kay Garnay, a cornerstone of Nepali culture is loosely translated, "What can I do?" The French say *que sera sera*. Speed, quality, anticipation, anything that resembles urgency, a sense of delaying gratification are <u>NOT</u> in the official Nepali handbook of fatalistic life.

Didn't finish a task? Didn't get started? Your whatzzit doesn't work? Kay Garnay, next life.

Except the food. Shriveled cows wander the streets uninhibited, mud is everywhere, the electricity goes on and off for hours, sometimes days at a time. Obtaining accurate, real time information is a chore yet order succulent chicken chili, pizza, omelets, delicious apple crumble with custard, mouth-watering pastries and bread to name a few, even during power brown-outs.

Why is this, Andy? With a huge smile, and his hands in the air in surrender, he clarified like someone who's been here awhile: "Read the posters...we're in *A Land of its Own*."

A local recognized Andy in a disparaging tone. Hinduism's strong *caste* system, a hereditary social ranking based on wealth, inherited rank, or occupation, is non-negotiable, and Andy's marriage to a woman of a lower caste limits him in the society. Mithu, capable and bright, could solve world hunger, end nuclear proliferation, and eradicate cancer but will forever bear the cross of the name into which she was born.

So what's a nice, white, urbane, traveled, Ivy League, upper-middle class, Wharton School of Business, Master's in Russian Literature, personal library owner filled with black & white framed pictures of Russian literary giants, All-American boy like Andy doing in a country that is, at times, leaping forward into the Fifteenth Century? He's not anti-American by any means but he's not a Nepali either. He's caught in some sort of middle ground, following his heart that says there are other things to do with his life than spend it chasing a gadget called The American Dream.

"I was destined to be an accountant, or Wall Street law," he mused. "Even now, my father, who was in the garment business for 50 years, calls from Florida and says that he can get me started in middle management at Wal-Mart. Only once did I wonder what I was doing here, in Nepal. I came into the house and heard some noises coming from the hallway. I swung open a closed door...there was a goat in my bathroom."

Kay Garnay.

WHITE KNUCKLE RAFTING
Ship of Fools Survives the Spills

"HIGH SIDE LEFT!!" bellowed Dave, the Scottish born chief. Trekking in Nepal didn't sound like such a hot idea but whitewater rafting did. A four day/three night rip down the *Kali Gandaki River* covered about 60 miles; mode of transportation - three inflatable Zodiac rafts, two for the 16 rafters and the third for supplies. I volunteered for the front, right position of the eight person crew, promised to be the splashiest post on the craft.

So why was Dave yelling like that? Because we had missed our lane running some fast current, and were wedged half sideways up a rock, partly crosscurrent and partly with. The river poured into the right side of the raft and spilled over top.

Dry-bags tightly roped in a grid fashion were heaped in the center of the raft. The right side crew members were to lay over to the left, re-distributing the weight balance, and hoping an undercutting current would lift us out of the jam.

"MOVE HIGHER...PUSH, PUSH, GET US OUT OF HERE!"

It wasn't working.

"JIM, TAKE YOUR MAN AND YANK THAT TIE ROPE AT THE FRONT *HARD*!"

My man, the front left paddler Anna, a woman from Iceland, and I pulled up on the mooring rope to lift the bow of the raft.

"RIGHT SIDE, PULL YOUR HANDLES ON THE SIDE OF THE RAFT AND LIFT! LEFT SIDE, LEAN OUT!"

Nothing. We were stuck.

These damn rafts need winches.

Three supervisors, experts of rivers and owners of the company, paddled along as safety kayakers. One found an eddy, stabilized himself from sweeping down the river, and yelled:

"THERE'S BLAH BLAH UNDER BLAH BLAH SIDE BLAH BLAH!"

The river splashed its hydro-orchestra. The kayaker moved in closer, paddling wildly as the safety of his eddy's perimeter weakened.

"THERE'S ANOTHER BLAH CAUGHT BLAHNEATH! HIGH SIDE RIGHT!"

"HIGH SIDE RIGHT?!" questioned Dave.

"HIGH SIDE RIGHT! DO IT!"

Another rock had us wedged in, which neither Dave or anyone else in the raft could see.

"HIGH SIDE RIGHT!" ordered Dave.

Rocking back and forth. The bow twisted then boomeranged back. Anna's knee landed in my ribs.

"GO BACK TO HIGH SIDE LEFT!"

This moved us a little.

"HIGH SIDE RIGHT!"

Bodies slammed back and forth. The floor of the raft convexed and screeched against the rock underneath. With the roar of the water in our ears and faces, we pitched from side to side, each shudder closer to freedom. Stu the kayaker nodded approvingly at Dave's leadership and our gradual success. A final liberating kick spun us from the high-centering snare and back into the rapids.

"Right side forward, left side back!" was the next command to straighten the craft. We beached to collect ourselves and survey for damage. Everything was in its right place. The next few hours passed meekly, and the first night's camping spot appeared.

Camping Under The Stars

Lodgings were at the glamorous Sandbar Hotel. Leaned-over rafts supported by paddles formed half an A-tent. Light nylon tarps, anchored by guy ropes tied to rocks, constructed the other wall. These accommodations housed five. A kitchen tent hosted most cooking then converted into a bunkhouse for the night. Most simply slept under the stars.

The guides, at the end of a three month training session, were under evaluation from the kayakers. Each day, two different leader-du-jours delegated tasks and made decisions.

A nylon outhouse was an essential edifice. A paddle dug a two foot pit and two flat rocks were positioned on each side of the hole for foot grip and to prevent the sides from caving in. A kick of sand served as a flush. Outside, the paddle was driven into the ground and crowned with a helmet, used as a vacancy indicator. On the ground meant the "coast was clear," on the paddle meant, "Occupied." Paper was put into a plastic bag and thrown in the garbage after packing up the tent the next morning - the last chore before setting out. The paddle refilled the hole and no one would ever know we were there.

Iodine added to a bucket of river water sat ten minutes to kill the bugs. Gravity fed the water through the attached spigot. The guides made a big deal about EVERYONE washing their hands with supplied *Dettol* soap.

A trench, with the sand piled as a backrest then upholstered further with life jackets, circled a fire-pit in a safe, central location. I was eating dinner next to Stu, another Scot, and the ultimate leader on our trip, leaning back and chatting about the day when something crawled up my forearm. I didn't feel alarmed and showed it to Stu.

He spoke sharply: "Don't move!" and deftly flicked it away. "Scorpion."

Another leader, John, a robust Australian with a bearded, weathered, sunned face, knew more campfire songs than a *Hearty Texas Stew* commercial, and, inspired by hot-rum punch, led the sing-a-longs around the ol' campfire well into each night.

That night delivered a terrible windstorm. I lay in my sleeping bag trying to invite sleep as the sand hoarded around any edge it could find. In the morning, a fine silt was in my ears, between my teeth, and up my nose. Breakfast crunched much more than scrambled eggs, toast, and hot chocolate should.

Back on the river, we passed phenomenal rock formations eroded smooth by millions of years of high monsoon waters and explored an abandoned royal palace in the middle of nowhere. Squawking birds competed with wild monkeys.

A village celebrating a wedding waved. Teenagers clambered over one another for the coveted position of receiving and hitching each raft's rope. Huge cauldrons of soup and vegetables bubbled on fires. Goats rotisseried slowly over smoldering coals. When we loaded up to leave, the adolescents own pushing and shoving distracted themselves to the point we untied our own ropes. After they saw their lost opportunity, they dove into the water and swam alongside, laughing, cackling, and friends again.

Over the four days, we faced five spots of *Class IV* whitewater, the most challenging for amateur rafters to tackle. Before each *Rumble in the Bubble*, the guides would preview from the shore, then brew up a game plan for the best route through.

The next day's first rapids, relatively mousy, claimed one crewmember, Kareen from Manhattan. She skidded over the rocks on her rapidly bruised buns until a safety kayaker zeroed in and guided her back to the raft. Three people pulled her back into the raft, then we were delayed again by her hyperventilating from laughing.

Rock n Roll

The most notorious rapids came the third day. Re-con ordered us to steer left of a huge rock in the middle of the river, paddle like crazy, hold on to hit a hole (water gains speed over a rock and drives under the natural level of the water, creating a "hole" in the river) get soaked, paddle out, hold on for another hole, get soaked again, then paddle out to the other side. As we drifted around the corner, the rock was easy to spot. The familiar roar grew.

"Left side forward," directed Anna from Switzerland. The left side paddled and the right side relaxed.

"All forward."

Our speed increased.

"All forward faster."

Water splashed over the bow into my face. I shook my head to clear my eyes and saw we were wrong.

"LEFT SIDE FORWARD, RIGHT SIDE BACK!!!!!!" she commanded. "LEFT SIDE DRAW!!!!!!"

The left side reaches out as far as possible and draws water in, perpendicular to the craft. The right side pushes out, using the boat as a fulcrum. At that speed, draw was a euphemism for fasten your seatbelt, or put another way, if the raft was a hospital, the draw command was the gurney into ICU. We never made it to the left. In fact, we were so far right of our landmark rock, for a moment, I thought I had heard the initial directions wrong. The rock passed quickly on the other side. A barricade of boulders was straight ahead.

"HOOOLD OOOONNN!!!!!"

I was hanging on before the mayday, we spun 180 degrees, the left side lurched up, I saw Heinz from Germany, front paddler on the left this day, thrown towards me, then the safety of the boat took leave from underneath. Literally and figuratively I held my breath, resigned to smashing against submerged rocks.

For some reason, I foolishly believed I was the only one out of the boat and it was passing over top. I stayed under as long as possible as everything transformed into the incredible sound of silence except for the bubbles of my exhaling. Thankfully, *bones versus stones* didn't arrive.

Resurfacing to assess the situation, I was in a calm eddy, the rocky shore a mere arm's-length away. The raft was upside-down, teetering on the dry-bag pile between two boulders, four other paddlers near, slightly shaken, but exhilarated. Oars seemed to be everywhere. Stu, the guide, was tiptoes on a boulder counting heads - ours plus those floating down the river. He held up nine fingers and shouted "Nine...I got nine heads!" and his shoulders relaxed.

The three of us who didn't wash down the river, together with Stu's guidance, heave-hoed the raft top side, dislodged it from the rocks, kicked it out and back into the stream, and paddled like hell through, with hoots and cheers from the others along with, by then, a large congregation of hill people.

The second and third rafts found their way through properly. When they saw our flip, neither was in a position to stop and beach. They described a slow motion dream, the raft lifting high on the right side then slowly lifting, lifting, lifting from the left and landing upside-down on the rocks.

We regained our crew, unanimously demanded forthwith that Anna stop apologizing, and continued on.

Deflated

The next morning, around the first bend, the water's persistent erosion over the centuries had eaten a cave into a sheer-faced cliff. Above the entrance, water sprinkled from the ends of long, stringy, green vines. Our *captain du jour*, Chris from England, steered us beneath this organic showerhead for the morning's ablution.

Shortly thereafter, we tried beaching to scout the next rapids but hit a sharp rock and punctured the raft. Heinz, sitting passively on the inflated gunwale, went straight backwards into the drink like a patsy in a charity dunk-tank. An hour later of equipment switching and repairs and on our way again, we decided to name our tub. The Titanic, The Poseidon, The S.S. Minnow tied for first. We felt we'd been through everything so the remainder of the day, coincidentally the last, would be clear sailing. Sorry to disappoint for there is no more drama. I was tired, sneezing, coughing, sick from four days of wet. Although the trip's chores were more work than I'd hoped, I was satisfied, but also happy to be going home to a hot shower, a cold beer, a soft bed, and a sit-down toilet.

The river had long stretches of calm parts and time for nasty water fights. Usually, a few splashes from an oar woke up a lethargic crew. This time, the other raft was beaking off six lengths away. One of their guys swam over and began an open daylight assault. Time for a countering commando raid. I dropped my paddle, leapt onto the dry bags, and dove in from this higher perch. The water was a bit murky, making my detection difficult as I stroked along. The home boat grew concerned for my whereabouts; the enemy only knew I dove in their direction. Heads oscillated, eyes focused, trying to catch a glimpse of me somewhere between the two vessels.

"Where is he...where is he?"

Swimming against the difficult current, my legs, arms, and chest, deprived of oxygen, began to burn. I dove deeper, under their boat to the far side, and initiated my rise to the surface. Gaining speed, the sunlight increased in intensity. Lifting out of the water like a submarine launched cruise missile, I reached for shoulder straps on the life jackets of two unsuspecting rivals looking the wrong way. I pulled myself up onto the raft, simultaneously sending them backwards to their watery tombs. I pounced to the rear and placed each hand onto the shoulders of Dave, the traitor now commanding this miscreant pack of seafarers, and pushed him to his own Davy Jones's Locker. Desperate hands lunged as I sprang to the top of their dry bags and plunged back into the river, corkscrewing in the air before submerging towards the safety of my home craft. The others, reeling from the lightning attack, wondered again, "Where could he be?" I again swam, this time with the current, deep to the other side of my safe-haven craft and quietly rose to the surface, detected only by those on that side. With a finger to my lips I negotiated for their silence, but snickers and giggles revealed my position.

"All forward," directed John from Upstate New York, who was in the saddle this day. "Jim...Jim...JIM! Get paddling...stop daydreaming!"

Ah, well, made for a good story anyway.

CONNECTING WITH STRANGERS MAKES TRAVELING <u>PRICELESS</u>

Varanasi, in the Indian state of Uttar Pradesh, is the typical hot and dusty mayhem. I arrived at the train station shortly after four headed to Calcutta. Consistent with Indian rail time, the train was indefinitely delayed. A few of us foreigners scavenged for air-conditioning in the tourist room.

"Are you here waiting for your trains? No, No, NO! GET OUT! This office is for only selling of tickets. Leave now!" screeched a ticket agent hereinafter referred to as Sweetheart of the Century.

I moved down the platform. Like the cloud of dust that followed Pigpen in Peanuts, the flies swarmed in a tidal wave rising above, wrapping over my head, and settling back behind to be replaced by more.

An Austrian man, eating oranges, waited on the platform. I bought a kilo and joined him. With his small bag of clothes and guitar, he had taken a bus from Vienna through Turkey, Iran, Pakistan, and into India; he was now heading back to Delhi to fly home to Europe. We made our way through a few more kilos, swapping stories, and shaking our heads at the immediate environment until his train pulled out.

Twain said, "Everyone is a moon, and has a dark side which he never shows to anybody." If the audience rejects who and what we are, we have nothing left to offer, making the stakes of this kind of gamble too high. Projecting a false front removes the peril; it's not real hence emotionless and expendable, sacrificed with no loss incurred.

Out in the wild blue yonder, a million miles from home, anyone who invariably judges us is restricted by the transitory nature of traveling. Wary at first, I probed for his plans. To discover he was soon on his way, in another direction, eased me. Now disarmed, it was safer to expose myself. Stating what was on my mind without fear of reprisal, and no threat to our temporary friendship, I tried new ideas and monitored his reaction. We had experienced many of the same highs and lows, and our conversation continually verified that he also had fears, weaknesses, strengths, and so on.

Does Your Meter Work?!

The opportunity to be approved of simply for what "dishes you bring to the pot-luck" is a self-discovery aspect of travel that should never be undersold or diminished. Traveling is the shooting range and these pseudo-friends are target practice.

Everyone has personal beacons to attract notice. The singular look in the other person's eye or the lilts of their voice effectively reveals if this person is a candidate to relate to and to what depth. Later, something triggers the memory of the person and their image is the link to remembering the before, during, and after that led up to the meeting, the image of their face already deposited in your memory bank. Cues are often added by relating something well known. The Austrian resembled Roger Daltrey, and his guitar was a glue to further summon the recollection. It's the same for all the others who come and go quickly while on the road, too numerous for all to be written about.

HOLY COW, INDIA FASCINATES

A teeming city with 1500 temples and mosques froths in the northern Indian state of Uttar Pradesh. It was originally called Kasi, meaning bright in Sanskrit, and nicknamed "The City of Light." Plundering medieval hordes corrupted the pronunciation of two local streams Varana and Asi into Baranas, which stood until the Indian government finally decreed the official name Varanasi in 1956. Eight miles away lies Sarnath where Buddha gave his first sermon after enlightenment and revealed the eight fold path to Nirvana. One of the holiest Hindu spots in India, a million pilgrims a year come to Varanasi, a tirtha (pilgrimage site), to purify by bathing in and drinking from the Ganges (from ganga, Sanskrit for river) River at sunrise.

An affable hotel clerk promised ground transportation and a boat to observe the shore scene from on the river: $3.50 round-trip. A 4:45 wake-up call arrived early. A teen goaded his cyclo through the quiet streets, winding through narrow, whiffy alleyways. Slight inclines in the road proved too steep for the youth to conquer, partly attributable to his age, partly to the disrepair of his vehicle, and mostly to fatigue. When unable to pedal, he jumped to the ground and gallantly pushed on. The still cool air, preparing to surrender to the day's arid heat of the Ganges Plain, blended the fetors of stale urine, rotting cow dung, and grime with the aromas of fresh bread, anise, curry, and jasmine.

From a doorway, the hotel clerk, like James Bond, stepped out with nary an expression. On foot, we snaked around ancient walkways until finally appearing on top of a three-mile stretch of ghats, (pass or mountain in Hindi), terraced stone steps leading down to the river. The just appearing sun blazed autumn auburn lasers across the still water.

An old, weathered man in a t-shirt and a colorless, faded sarong paddled a rickety canoe-like vessel down the river and then up. The young cyclo driver, still part of the full package, bailed. Twinkling in the dawn, cups with lit candles surrounded by red flowers floated past - a veneration to the gods.

Massive log piles stacked neatly back from the shoreline. At spots along the water's edge were three layers of logs piled in a criss-cross configuration. Between the logs, a white sheet veiled a

118

cadaver, its arms, feet, and head unmistakable. A final layer of wood covered the corpse, set for cremation, and a closing to the circle of life, in this holy place.

Bovines, and other animals, cruised the banks. Possible reasons for India's worship of the cow begin in Hindu scripture. One legend says that King Dilip offered himself to a lion in exchange for the cow's life of which he had tutelage. Such is the Hindu belief of regard for those under your care. Another explanation for the holy cow is respect for the giver of life, nourishment, and labor. Oxen pulled the ploughs and fed the people whose diets have used dairy products as a staple. Declaring bovines holy kept the milk tap running. Hindus revere all animals, and the cow is viewed as representative of all animals.

Meanwhile, in the playground of a river, men, women, and children of every age soaped themselves, brushed their teeth, painted their faces, washed, splashed, played, squealed. Some stood waist deep, their hands together, eyes closed in worship. Others ritualistically filled their ornate silver bowl with the exalted water and emptied it with a slow stream, their lips moving in muted prayer. Dhobi wallah, Indian laundry men, twisted and lumberjacked colorful clothing, heavy with detergent and water, against boulders lining the shoreline. Sun-dried clothes filled the ghats following the contours of the steps. Children played cricket with a stick and tennis ball.

The clerk waited at the point of insertion and offered a stop for breakfast and coffee. But first, a fight over baksheesh. Baksheesh is somewhere between a bribe and a tip, depending on the circumstance. The smiling boatman held out his left hand.

"Up to you," replied the clerk when I asked for guidance.

I reminded him of his $3.50 offer, all-inclusive. He had a shrug so good it was audible. By now, the scowling sailor's empty paw foreclosed all smiles. His right backhand smacked once, twice, three, four times his left palm. I knew all along what the situation represented.

"IT'S NOT MY FAULT YOU ARE SO POOR!" my insides screamed. My outsides walked away without a word. Varanasi, thousands of years later, lives on, steeped in history, life, death, and contradiction.

I'LL BET YOU DIDN'T KNOW THAT THE MACHIAVELLI FAMILY LOST A SON AT BIRTH AND IT RESURFACED AS A TICKET AGENT IN INDIA

To Travel the Trains in India, One Must Learn the Rules

The world's largest employer with more than 1.5 million employees is the Indian train system institution. To book a train ticket, air-conditioned tourist rooms for foreigners provide special help.

Four foreigners waited as the two agents chatted loudly, arrogantly ignoring those expecting service. The quieter of the two left and the other served an Israeli guy patiently sitting.

"What?" the vendor curtly solicited, lifting his chin sharply and pointing.

"I want a ticket to Calcutta."

"For when?"

"When can I go?"

"When do you want to go? Listen, if you don't know what you want then don't come here to waste my time. Go away and come back when you know what you are talking about."

I felt instantly intimidated.

"Can I go tomorrow?"

"You can go tomorrow," he snarled, checking his computer. Snapping all the way, he continued. "It will cost you 167 rupees ($1=35RP), 2nd class sleeper. It leaves at 4:30 in the afternoon. Show me your passport and bank receipts for traveler's checks."

"Oh, no," I thought.

The law states foreigners must prove they changed money in an official establishment but no one ever keeps account. I mean, I never did.

"I don't have my receipts..."

"You cannot have the tickets without producing the receipts," he barked, pointing at a sign on the wall.

"Yes, I know, but it would be better for me if you gave me the ticket..."

"Not without the bank receipts! It's the law in India!"

Does Your Meter Work?!

My heart sunk. Mr. Used Car Salesman, the clerk back at the guesthouse, hadn't provided any receipts when we traded traveler's checks. He knew that mentioning the regulation would spook a newly arrived rookie like me. It was late and I couldn't recall seeing any banks in that zoo of traffic and mayhem outside I was trying so hard to avoid.

"Yes I know," the Israeli continued, "I have the receipts at my hotel so it would be better for me if you could give me the ticket and I will come back with receipts."

"I'm sorry, no, you must have the receipts!"

I would have given up by now, but our hero, unfazed, continued on in a clear, even voice.

"But it would be better for me if you give me the ticket so I know..."

"No, impossible!"

The other foreigners, enjoying the spectacle, silently led the cheer. Back and forth the Israeli-Indian verbal cockfight went until, suddenly grinning, the ticket agent said Uncle and printed the ticket. Then almost daring the Israeli - it was clear now he had his finger on the pulse of Indian ways - to snatch the dangling voucher from his hand, the Indian said, in no uncertain terms,

"I will give you the ticket, BUT you must come back this evening or I will CANCEL the ticket!"

Israel's head nodded once on a slant, his eyes closing in syncromesh with grace, "No problem, I will come back." Calmly, he took his time folding and stowing away the papers while all eyes trained onto his every move. The ticket agent looked both at a loss and impressed.

Now it was my turn.

"I would like a ticket for Agra." The Taj Mahal is in Agra.

"Fine, the next spot available is four days from now."

"Oh," I said, trying to muster courage from the previous guy's example, "How about a ticket to Darjeeling?"

I heard him spit out something along the lines of: "to Darjeeling you take a train three days from now (*to some place I didn't understand*) then transfer to (*another place I didn't get*) and then take a bus to (*another place I didn't understand*). From there, take a taxi."

"Huh?" I responded intelligently and astutely.

He lifted his eyebrows and tilted his head, like a boxer or a guy at closing time, saying, "Take your best punch."

I was too afraid to ask for clarification of the body language or the directions. My head reeled from the dialogue.

Feigning composure, I shifted gears. "I see. Are there any more tickets to Calcutta tomorrow?"

He blew a gasket. Throwing his pen down, sitting back in his chair, crossing his arms, and with his head bobbing up and down in time with his words, he cried,

"Where do you want to go, man? How am I supposed to know what to do for you unless you tell me?"

I flushed.

"Okay, okay, can you give me a 2nd class sleeper for Calcutta tomorrow?"

"167 rupees. Show me your passport and bank receipts."

"I didn't bring … receipts, they are back in my hotel and I can..."

Ears perked.

"You guys think you can get away with this not having receipts. It is the law of India to show where you have changed your money because of problems of the black market. When you come to our country you must follow the rules...I will give you the ticket but both of you must bring in the receipts or I promise I will CANCEL the spaces," he ranted, scowling and then just as quickly, just as convincingly, suddenly smiling.

Israel was staying at the same hotel as me. Later that evening, I asked him what he was planning to do about the long lost receipts.

"The train guy can go to hell," he snorted through his accent.

I arrived at the train station shortly after four the next day. Consistent with Indian railroad timetabling, the train was indefinitely delayed. A few of the train-lorn foreigners scavenged for air-conditioning in the tourist room.

"Are you here waiting for your trains? No, No, NO! GET OUT! This office is for only selling of tickets! Leave now!!" screeched Mr. McMonster.

I walked to the platform and the posted passenger list. There it was, J. Soliski. Behind me, I sensed someone close. It was

Does Your Meter Work?!

Israel. His expressionless face and James Dean cool nodded and closed his eyes, once, when I asked if he saw his name.

Life got easier in India.

SRI LANKA

"Where are you going, sir?"

"I want to go to Fort. Is this where the bus stops?"

"I'm sorry, sir, very few buses go to Fort. You will be waiting a long time. You should take a taxi."

"No, that's okay, I'll wait. Is it here where the bus stops?"

"No sir, it's on the other side and down the road past that corner. Can I take you there?"

"No, but thanks for your help."

The taxi driver turned and drove back to the guarded entrance of the airport where his buddies lurked. Another unsolicited taxi stopped.

"I don't want a taxi but can you tell me where the bus stops for Fort?"

"It is on this side of the road," he advised.

Now I really didn't know whom to believe. A bus approached. The driver said no for Fort, but confirmed the side of the road where my feet rested was indeed where they should stay.

Counting touchdown, I'd been in Sri Lanka approximately half an hour and I liked it already. The few people I'd come in contact with had a decidedly gentler demeanor than in India. Even the hack hustler trying to give me a ride cut it out quickly, although his wild goose chase crack didn't promote humanity.

My bus soon pulled up, the wait long enough to be ogled at by everyone who passed by. Rather empty at first, three or four stops converted the bus into one of the top few most densely populated spots on Earth. Passengers hung outside the door like silverware in a full dishwasher as we roared down the street, the outermost hung on with one hand and one foot waving in space. WHOMP! went one of the worn tires, followed by a pack of groans. The driver and purser engaged in rousing discussion until the latter deserted. The former handed back refunds. Like a goober, I patiently waited thinking some resemblance to order would follow, but soon realized aggression was the only way to avoid being the final one refunded. The mob, like reporters planting microphones in Michael Jordan's face, stuck their ticket stubs into the driver's immediate field of vision and yelled a lot. I slowly maneuvered my stub closer and closer until it touched his hands. He served us in a quasi-logical pattern, but each time my turn should have arisen, he passed over my distinctively alabaster fist until only I remained to be paid. I didn't get the impression it was a racist tactic, rather I assumed that the driver wanted to be sure he had enough money to reimburse everyone. In the event of a shortfall, nothing would have come out of his jeans; I was implicitly voted the most likely able to absorb the six rupee (10 cents) debit.

The others dispersed and I waited for another bus with Fort indicated as its final stop. Typically, I drew long stares.

Fort, an hour from the airport, is the original district of Colombo where the British had set up shop during their plundering days. These days, it's the downtown area. Busy streets, a few big hotels, a waterfront park, Buddhist shrines, and lots of army.

One proposed possibility where Colombo derives its name is *kola*, which means *leaves* and *amba* means *mango*. Another possibility comes from an old Sinhalese word *kolamba*, which is *port* or *ferry*. Sinhalese is the primary language spoken in Sri Lanka. Sri Lanka derives from Sanskrit *shri*, happiness or holiness and *lanka*, island or translated as *Island of the Blessed*.

I found a room at *The Ex-Servicemen's Institute*, a classic in bottom-of-the-line digs. The interesting plank floors were slippery from years of wear. My room was so narrow, I couldn't fully stretch my arms across without hitting the walls. A slender cot, a desk and chair, and a wooden rack to set my bag completed the decor. In rows of eight, paper-thin walls reached halfway to a high ceiling. The top half of the wall was mesh to facilitate circulation. At night, one light left on shone across all the rooms. Without all the fans whirling, it was a sauna.

Speaking of steamy, I laid on my cot sweating while partners alternated on either side of me trying to orgasm in silence. When something pleasurable required a groan, a poorly camouflaged clearing of the throat didn't fool anyone. The ladies weakly masqueraded giggles indicated a pushing of the right buttons. Wobbly old beds creaking in time to thrusts presented the lovers' biggest challenge to silence. Appetite defeated modesty as they built up to climax and tried to adjust positions to keep the bed's noise to a minimum. One bloke tried valiantly to cover the squeaking by speaking in a natural tone, as he and his partner reached their separate heights of ecstasy.

Does Your Meter Work?!

Colombo is an agreeable city. It's core, Fort, is only a few blocks square. Unfortunately, since the early 1980's, the Tamil Tigers and the Sri Lankan government have been in the middle of a grueling, tiring civil war. Lovely Palladian architecture from British days made for decent photography, but many buildings are bunkered and razor-wired off. As I lined up the first photo, a soldier ran across the street and politely asked that I avoid taking pictures of any government buildings. He readily agreed to have his picture taken, and under this ruse, I bypassed his mug in the viewfinder and snapped the building in the background.

Later, walking elsewhere, I stopped and stood for a moment to calibrate my bearings with those of a map. A strange noise came from somewhere. From across the street. Two soldiers, gun barrels poking from within a pillbox, clapped their hands seeking my attention. "Walk! Walk!" they ordered. I resumed and soon located on the map that I had stopped in front of the prime minister's official residence.

At night, the nearby Hilton Hotel generated some noise and a half-block stretch of soup-stands revealed life otherwise the streets were so quiet, I thought The Beatles were back on Ed Sullivan. To my surprise, I turned a corner and saw, like bees hovering at the entrance to their nest, a group of 20 or so men milling about an otherwise dark, deserted street. They spoke softly, occasionally bursting with screeches, and waving their hands in the air. Curiosity directed I approach from the opposite side to investigate. The attraction was, what else, a television in a store window broadcasting the cricket match between Good Old Ourside and India. I moved in to ask the score and a couple other cricket-appropriate questions. This tired soon and I continued on my exploration. Each time Sri Lanka hit a four or a six (roughly equivalent to a home run in baseball), muffled cheers spread from behind closed windows or from upstairs quarters.

Every block, auto-rickshaw drivers pressed hard for the chance to introduce me to some Sri Lankan ladies. The pimps all opened at 800 rupees ($13.33) for "an hour of very good service, sir," instantly dropped to 700 after my first refusal, and wouldn't go any lower as I made tracks. For price shoppers, 700 was apparently the bottom line.

Does Your Meter Work?!

A strange guy summoned me over. I didn't go so he skipped up.

"Where you from?" he wanted to know.

"Japan, where does it look like?" I shot back, "where you from?"

He looked at me like I was daft.

"Colombo...I take you around, show you everything." He waved his scruffy arms in the air. "You don't pay me anything."

"I don't need you to show me around. No thanks. Anyway...no money."

"You don't live here. I must show you what to do. You don't pay me."

"And I don't believe you. Go away." I turned and went from whence I came.

He caught up.

"I show you, I show you."

"Get lost."

I beetled across the street and continued walking. He followed along on his side. I turned and went the other way. He mirrored my steps. I saw an empty can and threw it at him. Missed by a mile. I walked again. He shadowed each step. The effective deterrent missing all this time were the four rocks I should have picked up in the first place. He hoofed it down the street and peeked out from the safety of the other side of a building corner.

Walking home, with the ammunition still in my hands, a squad of stray dogs barked threats from among rips in a steel fabricated fence. Behind was an empty lot. I raised my hand in defiance. They snarled louder. I hurled a stone, missed the closest pooch, but hit the steel. The sharp CRACK! scared the bejabbers out of the canine gang. Instead of running to relative safety, they sprinted to where I was able to unleash the full might of my ordnance, clipping one on the rear. He yelped, I breathed.

The next day, the bus depot was part of a busy, crowded market area. I spent nearly an hour trying to find the bus to Kandy, a small city a couple hours north. No less than seven people claimed to know the correct number on the bus and pointed directions to the pick up point. Each time I confirmed with the drivers, they either said, "Wrong bus" or "I don't know." Something was amiss, ajar, a conspiracy in the alignment of the stars. Maybe I should of checked for a full moon later that evening.

Kandy, or *Kandha*, Sinhalese for *mountain*, sits at an elevation of 1600 feet in lush jungle, streams, and wildlife. The cooler temperatures made sleeping much more comfortable.

My hotel was the Olde Empire Hotel. Long, thick, solid planks, smoothed and varnished, constructed the floors. The double-doors swung into the room like a grandiose Hollywood entrance. Sheer curtains hung over the windows. My bed had sweeping arcs where a mosquito net substituted for a veil in this Arabian prince's boudoir; going rate, 272 SLR ($4.50). The hallways, decorated with local art and beautiful vases full of fresh flowers, led to a common balcony to view a man-made lake, which the city centered around. Hanging lazily, branches of huge trees surrounding the water pacified the sidewalk. A small island, originally built to keep the king's concubines, became an ammunition dump when the British arrived. Now, its part of the decor.

The Temple of the Tooth is Kandy's major attraction. One of three places in the world reportedly containing a tooth belonging to Buddha himself, the denture is housed in a small box that is not for public viewing. Faith is required to believe the tooth belonged to Buddha and whether there actually is a tooth inside the box. All I know is I saved two dollars on the entrance fee by bribing through the independent security check for the grand total of two cigarettes.

Kandy is dandy as a place to visit and hang out. A tout named Nelson, who always seemed to pop up wherever I went, had become friendly and guided me around for a day.

First stop was a farm with four trained elephants. Elephants have played an important role in this part of the world, not only through work but also spiritually. The 63-year-old patriarch of the crew had enormous tusks that almost dragged on the ground. His trunk, spotted pink, exposed the layer of skin under his thick hide. He bumped up against a dock like a mammal passenger ferry where I jumped on barefoot and clung to the chain wrapped around his neck. My groins stretched straddling his rock-hard vertebrae. His thick, scouring-pad hide scratched the inside of my thighs. His mass so overwhelmed mine I was grateful for his unruffled demeanor.

Does Your Meter Work?!

After my less than glorious dismount, his performance continued. He obeyed his trainer's commands by scooping logs under his tusks and holding them in place with that enormous trunk. Then, after a tough day at the office, he bathed himself by lying in a river and self-showering the morning heat and dust away. A natural ham, he posed for pictures, and then went back to what the other elephants do when not entertaining -- standing.

A botanical gardens featured quiet walks among a potpourri of indigenous flora. Thousands of daytime bats the size of seagulls clutched upside down to trees until someone volunteered, for a fee, to rattle their cage. The rattler found an old stick and banged on the trunks. Skittish by nature, the slumbering bats had no resilience to this man's thrashings and flew their coops, blocking out the sun, and formed foreboding moving shadows like the Air Cavalry was in town.

Nelson decided he'd had enough and bid goodbye. A decent middle-aged man, 80% grayed, and a heckuva grin, he had only asked that his bus tickets and admissions be paid.

A solo hike through an animal sanctuary among hills that rise behind my hotel ended the day. The cooler altitude and thickness of the vegetation blocked the sun so thoroughly I felt a chill. The only animals were hordes of monkeys disinterested in the people and more interested in indiscriminate copulation. "Monkey business in its purest," I theorized, then wondered, "Is everyone and everything in Sri Lanka having sex but me?"

When I arrived back in Colombo and headed to the hotel, I walked the exact same route with a differing mood from the first day in Sri Lanka. I exuded a peacefulness -- even a cockiness -- as I knew where to get off, where to go, and knew the route and distance from the bus stop to the hotel. The Ex-Servicemen's Institute, be it ever so humble, was the cheapest place in town.

JEWEL FOOL

Simple jewelry shops lined the street in front of my hotel. Sri Lanka has some of the highest quality gems in the world, particularly rubies. It also has some of the most talented scam artists on the planet. A slight man with tousled hair and old clothes waved.

"How are you today, my friend?"

I didn't know we knew each other. Silly me.

"Never better. How's yourself?"

"I'm very well, my friend. Please come into my shop. I have gems, the best in the world."

"Nah, I don't think so."

"Oh, sir, you must come in and look. It doesn't cost anything to have a look at what I have."

"I don't have any money, I'm a broke tourist."

"That is no problem, sir. You don't need to have any money. I can see you are a businessman. Please come in, you *must* come in."

This guy was only missing white shoes, wide lapels, and seersucker pants. I had to indulge his offer.

"Please, sir, sit down. Look at what I have. Diamonds, sapphires, blue sapphires, rubies, emeralds. Here is my certification as a registered and trained gemologist."

He pointed to a dog-eared, faded, yellow piece of paper thumbtacked onto the wall.

"Do you like rubies?" he started his probe.

"Don't know anything about them. They're bright red, right?" I said, letting out some line.

His eyes glinted like Hawkeye in M*A*S*H when a new poker player arrived in camp.

"Where else have you traveled to?" he asked.

"India, Nepal, South East Asia before that...I taught English in Taiwan last year."

"Do tell..." spoke my inquisitor's face. One of my Taiwanese students was in the jewelry business and he had been to Sri Lanka. The Taiwanese are big spenders when abroad.

"Are you going back to Taiwan soon?" he rummaged with a fresher politeness in his voice.

"I don't know, I don't have any reason to go back."

"Listen, close the door."

"It's hot in here."

"I will turn on the fan."

Closing the door darkened the room. He flicked on the light and forgot the fan.

"If you think you will go back to Taiwan soon I think you and I can do some very good business together. You can make a lot of money and it won't cost you anything."

His syrupy voice was giving me diabetes.

"Really, how can I do that?"

"Should you go back to Taiwan, or Hong Kong, Singapore...these are good countries too...you can take some of my rubies and sell them there. Oh yes, you can sell them for thousands of US dollars and make yourself some nice money."

"How much would I get for the rubies?"

"You could get *thousands*," he promised, his eyes bulging.

"How much are the rubies from you?"

"You don't have to give me anything," he answered, feigning insult. "I will give you these rubies and you take them with you. When you sell them, then you send me 20 per cent of your sale."

"How do I send you the money?"

"Simple, my friend. How long will you stay in Sri Lanka?"

"Dunno, not long, maybe ten days."

"Before you leave, I will give you my bank account number and, after you sell the rubies, you can send the money to me." He finished with his palms out and facing up. His grin was so big and soppy, the shop suddenly felt crowded.

"And you would let me take them without paying for them first?"

"Of course! I can see you are a businessman."

The air was getting stale and his modest proposal a little thick. Sweat ran down my neck and formed a stream along my spine. I wiped my face on my sleeve.

"Well, listen, that sounds like it has possibilities but I just arrived in Sri Lanka today and I don't know my plans yet. I'm staying near here and I know I'll see you again. It's really hot in here, isn't it? You don't want to turn on the fan?"

"Oh, I'm sorry sir, it doesn't work."

"Uh huh. I'll see you again but right now I'm really cooking and I want to go walk around a bit. Thank you for the information. Colombo looks really nice," I waxed lyrically as I stood up to leave.

"Oh yes, Sri Lanka is a very beautiful country. Do you need to change any money? I can do that for you now if you'd like?"

"I'm good on cash for now, I changed some at the airport."

"Be sure to come to me when it is money that you need. When you need money, come to *me*. I can give you better than the banks."

"I'm sure you can," I said, but thought: "I'm sure I won't" then turned to emancipate myself.

His speech sounded so good, flawless, in fact. What could go wrong with taking the stones on consignment and never sending the money? The catch was the jewels were glass or plastic. Any price was pure profit. But there had to be more to the story yet to be revealed. Months back, an amateur fortune-hunter had told me he got taken for $2800 in India during an identical scam, and the memory of that conversation left me smiling as I escaped down the street.

NOT MY WAR

Colombo, Sri Lanka, is an agreeable city. Unfortunately, since the early 1980's, the Tamil Tigers and the Sri Lankan government have been locked together in a grueling, tiring civil war. Lovely Palladian architecture from British colonial times contributes to the downtown area, but many buildings are bunkered and razor-wired off. Photography not permitted

While I was on a bus, a security check halted our progress. Passengers were ordered to line up on the sidewalk, produce I.D., encounter scrutiny, then move to another area, like an *IN* and *OUT* basket of humanity. I remained on the bus, alone, lacking any urge to become involved. A soldier in full battle gear saw the lone figure sitting inside the assumed deserted bus and boarded to inspect. His face carried surprise at seeing the spectacle of me in there, against orders, and then his look of shock changed to serious. The military figure was turning bureaucratic in front of my eyes. But he still had enough weaponry and ordnance to revert back to his army roots in a single heartbeat.

"You have identification?"

The day before, I had left my fully stamped passport in the Canadian embassy to have pages added. The embassy photocopied page one and the entry visa. I handed the trooper the xerox.

"You have no passport?"

"It's in the Canadian embassy getting more pages. They gave me this."

He didn't seem to like this answer and stood a few seconds in leery silence, then his expression switched to uncertainty, most likely trying to settle in his mind if my presentation represented terrorism. His eyes moved the length of my body stopping at my size 10 1/2's. They intrigued him, probably because of their size, huge by Asian standards. His gaze shifted from my feet to my bag on the floor to the black shoulder bag clutched tightly on my lap and back to my eyes. It felt like a showdown in a cowboy saloon, but then I sensed that he concluded I looked innocent enough. But what page of the army manual covered misplaced Caucasian cargo? What path to take, which uniform and hat to wear.

Does Your Meter Work?!

Two years of criss-crossing Asia left me confident that my shrug had progressed to the point of competing with the best. I lifted my shoulders up and down in the universal shrug of the weak and unofficial, and exposed my position:

"Not my war."

This pulled him out of his contemplation. He glanced at the paper once more, as if it held some answer for him, some clue to behavior under arms in a bus and, his face doing angry like I previously thought only Pacino could, dropped the unfolded voucher in my lap. The soldier turned smartly and exited the empty bus in silence.

The hush continued as I sat there sweating in the uncirculating equatorial heat now wondering by how much I'd just dodged a bullet.

<u>CRAPPY TRAVELING</u>

Number Two. Shit. Poop. Kaka. The French say *merde.* Translated literally in Mandarin, it's *big convenient. Guano,* the combined faeces from birds and bats, derives from *huanu*, which derived from Quechua, a South American Indian language meaning fertilizer dung. Anyway you say it, it's a topic, especially when traveling. After two years of "solid" traveling throughout Asia, every stop was an adventure.

Asia is famous for squat toilets, which Westerners stoop to conquer. Orientals find sit-down toilets equally eccentric. I walked my grumbling guts into the bathroom of a busy Taipei McDonalds where I knew to find sit-down toilets. It smelled a bit ripe but that's hardly news in Taiwan. I swung open the cubicle and the smell hit like a ton of fermented tofu. Footprints on the porcelain gave away that someone had squatted on the rim, then I saw that the owner of the prints also left behind a deposit - except his crosshairs shot high and to the right meaning a direct hit onto the rim. Half dripped into the bowl, the other half onto the floor. A dull peak rose less than majestically in the middle. I backed out slowly then took the time to walk over to The Hilton.

While whitewater rafting in Nepal, we camped on sand bars where a nylon outhouse was an essential edifice. A paddle dug a three-foot pit and two flat rocks were positioned on each side of the hole for foot grip and to prevent the sides from caving in. A kick of sand over the most recent deposit sufficed as a flush. Outside, the paddle was driven into the ground crowned with a helmet, used as a vacancy indicator. On the ground meant the "coast was clear," on the paddle meant, "Occupied." Paper was put into a plastic bag and thrown in the garbage after packing up the tent the next morning - the last chore before setting out. The hole was refilled and no one would ever have known we were there.

In the jungles of Borneo sits Niah Cave where millions of sleeping bats inhabit the cave by day. By night, with the bats out playing, a like number of swallows dwell in their nests, of which the Chinese harvest to make their famous bird's nest soup. The cave floor, thick with guano - the combined faeces of the cave's occupants - is carted away and sold for fertilizer. Armed guards protect the gathering areas.

The Moc Bai border crossing from Cambodia into Vietnam makes a great picture. A sign, a wide, sweeping arc over the first building says *VIETNAM* in a pastel blue. Policemen, in their distinctive olive-green uniforms, flat-top hat with a bright red band, and a disinterested look about their carriage said *communism*. Also, just as distinctive, is a sign saying, in English, *NO PICTURES*. I needed a bathroom and was directed to a too low, too tiny bamboo frame covered in tattered nylon cloth. The toilet was a concrete slab with a hole chipped out about the size of a softball. On either side of the opening sat a red construction brick to place your feet when squatting. Intestinal output splattered the immediate area. They were classy enough to supply toilet paper - torn pieces of newspaper in a box. I made two decisions. The first, to suffer the stomach cramps until Saigon, the second, they'd have been smarter to lose the war.

TOO MUCH GARLIC IS NEVER ENOUGH AND OTHER LUNCH <u>ADVENTURES IN ASIA</u>

Sweet and sour sauce is an invention to cater to Western tastes because authentic, everyday Chinese food starts and ends with the meat or vegetable, heaps of oil, a pile of MSG, and too much garlic. Sear quickly over a high heat. Once, while in a Taiwanese market buying groceries to make dinner, I selected some tomatoes, cabbage, bok choy, Chinese broccoli, some other greens, and an onion. I handed them to the old woman - with a wrinkled face and five teeth - to be weighed and put into a bag. Then I saw her huge basket of garlic and flashed three fingers, assuming three cloves. She dove her craggy hand in and began filling a bag. For her, three fingers could only have meant three kilos. Protesting, I corrected her by picking three cloves within her full view and put them in the bag, already full with the other vegetables. Her eyes bulged in shock. Collecting herself, she broke out in laughter. Saying *san-ge, san-ge* (*three-three* in Mandarin) she announced to those around her in the busy market what a goofy customer she had. What was I going to cook with only three cloves of garlic? She then gestured, "no charge for the garlic, ya goober." An assembly gathered, laughing, looking around to confirm that others were laughing too, rolling back and forth on their heels like people do when they feel the sanctity of safe surroundings, and probably saying, "We'll never forget this one, huh? What an ancestral anecdote to pass down to our descendants."

Nearly everyone in Malaysia eats with their hands. They mix their rice with sauces, swirl it around, scoop some in cupped fingers, and shovel it in. They swirl and mix again like icing a cake and shovel in some more. The restaurant staff catered to my Westernness by bringing a fork and spoon. Bowls of bananas for dessert scattered around the mess-hall layout. Against a wall was a sink to clean up. Above the mirror read "NO SPITTING." This evening's victuals were chicken curry and fish. I faced an assembly line of people, each person in charge of one dish. One put a big banana leaf as a plate on the table, a splurtch of rice followed, then chicken from a big pot, some fish, cooked cabbage, and a green vegetable. Service duration <15 seconds. First time for everything, service at the speed of light and a feast off a banana leaf.

Vietnamese cooking, influenced by the Chinese and French, is superb except for the overdoses of MSG, which can be a buzz. Diner-type restaurants in Vietnam display 10 to 35 different choices where a few well placed points of the finger offer something new at each meal. A little experimentation eventually whittles down the picks acceptable to the palate. Some choices simply look too bizarre to try. Two meats, a vegetable, rice, some salad, and iced tea cost anywhere from $1.50 to $2. Any Board of Health food inspector would close down every restaurant on preparation and storage infractions; nevertheless, anything more than the mild Saigon Shuffle or the occasional cramping is rare.

Potential trouble derives from etiquette more than the cooks. Fish skeletons, pork chop bones, fat, greasy paper napkins, rice, anything unwanted is not set onto the edge of the plate or even somewhere on the table, but spit onto the floor. The crew sweeps the debris onto hand shovels and tosses it onto the street to rot in the tropical sun. After the day's cars, bikes and pedestrians mix and mash, street sweepers working at night with extra long bamboo brooms gather and deposit it into handcarts among feeding rats and cockroaches. Daytime temperatures are always in the mid-90's, the ideal heat for bacteria to grow. Add casual urinating, spitting, littering, and a land unaware or unobliging to the concept of hygiene, it's horrifying to imagine the cocktail of germs that brews daily on that asphalt frying pan.

To minimize the Ho Chi Minh Trail to the bathroom, look for foods that are either cold or hot, outside the danger zone of temperature. Hot soup, or any meat over coals that go straight to your plate, or better yet, mouth, should be too hot for tummy greeblies to gestate. Other tips include: Make sure you're healthy before traveling. Try to eat at meal times so food is fresher. Wash your hands using soap and running water as often as is feasible, but don't become a neurotic. If something appears undercooked, don't eat it. Seafood is the most vulnerable to spoiling. Always drink bottled water, and ensure the seal is intact.

Ask your doctor for a prescription for Imodium (Loperamide) to halt diarrhea, and Buscopan (Hyoscine), a smooth muscle relaxant that eases cramping. Runny stools with blood and/or mucous means trouble. As does fever. Seek a doctor immediately. Above all, don't live scared! If one of those germs wants in, it'll find you. Use common sense, trust your eyes and instincts, and be sure to treat yourself to the cooking from wherever you go, as eating is one of the truly great returns of travel.

Also in Vietnam, Pho Ga (pronounced like "phaw-guh", *Pho* is a type of noodle and *Ga* is chicken) is THE bowl of chicken noodle soup of your life. A big bowl of noodles, chunks of shredded chicken, and a rich broth is brought to a table already crowded with containers of chilies, branches of mint leaves, another green leaf, bean sprouts, chili sauce, a bar-b-que sauce, and fresh lemon wedges; season to taste. At the best joint in Saigon, wobbly stools ring the restaurant's six equally wobbly wooden tables. The operators, a husband and wife and a mother (who wore the second hat of mother-in-law. We constantly discussed which spouse was her child and never found the answer) simmer their soup in a huge pot blackened over time from the smoke of the heat source, a contained campfire. Boiled chickens hang like Christmas decorations. They can't speak English, their foreign customers can't speak Vietnamese, yet while paying, both sides always seem to say thank-you in the other's language.

HAND IT TO MANKIND, THEY'VE LEARNED TO <u>COMMUNICATE</u>

In the Philippines, cock fighting is the indigenous passion among men. With some arenas holding up to thousands of spectators, an evolved series of hand gestures between bettors determines wagers. Holding fingers straight up indicates denominations of 10's, holding fingers sideways is for 100's, and pointing the corresponding amount straight down is for 1000's of pesos, of which there is no shortage. A bet of 1,350 pesos requires three movements. In the first, one finger points straight down, signifying "one thousand." Immediately three fingers extend horizontally, to signify "three hundred." Finally, all five digits point up, for five times ten, or fifty. A wave of the hand to the left or right indicates which foul fowl - busy in the ring getting mad - the bettor wants. Odds are set using another round of elaborate finger semaphore that only those with Filipino DNA can understand.

In Taiwan, when someone wraps their left hand around their right clenched fist, holds it tight at eye level, and proclaims, "LEE HI," you've done something worth veneration. When numbers are used during conversation, the right hand itself counts one to nine. One to five is each digit. Six is the thumb and pinky sticking out from a fist (the same gesture means "hang loose" in Hawaii). Seven is the thumb and forefinger, like a pistol. Eight is the thumb, forefinger, and middle finger. Nine is the thumb and first three fingers. Lightly touching forefinger tips means ten. Tapping the tabletop with one or two fingers means "Thank you."

In Vietnam, a vertical open palm and fingers spread apart, then frantically rotated back and forth three times means "No, I don't want, we don't have what you want, I don't know, etc."

Nepalis hold pressed palms together in front of their face, and slightly bow while saying, "Namaste" during introductions and greetings.

Koreans rub their palms together to ask, "Forgive me."

Does Your Meter Work?!

Westerners have a thumb, forefinger, middle finger, ring finger, and pinky. The Japanese dub them father finger, mother finger, brother finger, sister finger, and baby finger.

DID YOU KNOW THAT TRANSLATED LITERALLY INTO <u>MANDARIN...</u>

Hotel	is	Rice House
Train	is	Fire Car
Taxi	is	Counting Distance Car
Bus	is	Public Car
Zoo	is	Animal Garden
The Spout On Your Sink	is	Water Dragon's Neck
Elvis Presley	is	Cat King
Hong Kong	is	Fragrant Harbor
January	is	One Moon
February	is	Two Moon...and so on
Monday	is	Week One
Tuesday	is	Week Two...and so on except
Sunday	is	Week Heaven
Television	is	Electric Viewing Machine
Telephone	is	Electric Talk
Movie	is	Electric Picture
Light Bulb	is	Electric Bubble
Fax	is	Delivery Real Machine

Does Your Meter Work?!

Cell Phone	is	Big Brother Big
Gratuity	is	Little Fee
Umbrella	is	Rain Parachute
Skyscraper	is	Big Storey
Szechuan	is	Four Rivers
Tienanmien Square	is	Heavenly Peaceful Door
Pee	is	Small Convenient
Poop	is	Big Convenient
Potato	is	Soil Bean
Pasta	is	Italy Noodle
Lobster	is	Dragon Shrimp
Cabbage	is	Big White Vegetable
Beijing	is	North Capital
Tokyo	is	East Capital
America	is	Beautiful Country
China	is	Middle Country
France	is	Law Country

And In Japanese, Ichi Ban Means Number 1!

IGUACU FALLS
The Niagara on Viagra

The borders of Argentina and Brazil, where they meet up with Paraguay's, literally pour into each other at a rate of 5,000 cubic meters of water per second, depending on recent rains.

Iguacu Falls, mostly in Argentina, partly in Brazil, are the highlight of Iguacu National Park, a 385,000 square miles of ecological sanctuary and home to 2,000 species of plants, 450 bird species, more than 80 different types of mammals, and too many insect species to have counted them all yet.

Busy place.

Guarani Indian legend says that Iguacu Falls formed when a jealous forest god, who was enraged at a warrior escaping downriver with a contraband young girl in a canoe, caused the river's bed to collapse in front of the lovers. The girl plunged over the edge and turned to stone. The warrior survived as a lovelorn tree overlooking his vanquished betrothed.

Geologically speaking, the story lacks the romanticism. The conflux of Brazil's Rio Iguacu (Iguacu River) and Rio Parana (Parana River) tumbles over a basalt plateau, dividing into fingers, or *cataratas*, of water in numbers and force that indeed prevents any antediluvian purists remaining out there to deny gravity's existence.

At the entrance to the park, the well-organized and helpful multilingual staff hand out pamphlets and steer visitors to museums and displays that provide a quick lay of the land. Afterwards, the first quest for water from this human divining rod began by boarding a Disneyland-like choo-choo that filed through the jungle. Along the way, flocks as big as 20 butterflies flittered and danced, playing and leaping like dry land winged dolphins. Each flock matched brilliantly. One team was decorated primarily canary yellow with vermilion garnitures. Another was two-toned blue, sky and navy, and tastefully trimmed with a jot of white.

144

Does Your Meter Work?!

At the end of the line, a half-mile walk over sturdy steel catwalks spans benign murky rivers lined with more verdant jungle. Posted are picture signposts of "Don't feed the monkeys," "Stay clear of the snakes," and "Beware of jaguars."

As one draws nearer, the fall's most fearsome precipice lets out a few warnings. On the horizon, plumes of haze snort through gaps between trees. A dull growl increases in decibels with each step. The sound is consistent lacking bursts or drops. The humidity thickens. Steadily the growl turns to roar. A mushroom cloud of mist shot high then dissipated from wind. People could be seen turning for protection, moving back, and running away.

Finally, the source of all the fuss was in full view, and that forest god was some jealous. The Garganta del Diablo, or Devil's Throat, is a semi-circular bowl hundreds of yards across that deluges Noahesque quantities of river 250 feet into a cauldron of hissing mist so thick, a view of the bottom is only sporadically granted.

The volume of water is so great some seems too impatient to join the main push. Instead it flanks to either side and finds its own outlets over clusters of rock. Grasses that had grown tall at a drier time of year are now helpless to the stampede of fluid.

Billows of mist climbed high again and again, at times blowing back over all the expensive cameras. The shutterbugs turned for protection, moved back, or ran away.

Occasionally the sun would peek through on this cloudy day permitting an angel to offer a rainbow deep in the larynx of the Devil, but he quickly grew testy and pulled the blind on the porthole. Milton endures. Beelzebub sneers, "Keep your olive branches."

With Hydro Hades implacable, a retreat to the train backtracked to Cataratas Station for a sandwich and the beginning of a walking tour to the remainder of the falls. Perhaps they will be more of a puppy.

Does Your Meter Work?!

A flat stroll along jungle paths was a delight. Three monkeys auditioned for a new Olympic sport; tree gymnastics. The show lasted a couple of minutes, but humans proved a frightfully boring creature to the performers, so they decided another part of the jungle held greater allures and disappeared into the foliage.

Three barely visible ants were making off with unlikely carrion. Somehow they huffed and puffed and dragged a dead beetle on its back, surely 20 times higher in weight class, across the path to a chop shop for ants. This Volkswagen was too big to fit down any hole those tiny carjackers would dig. Squads of butterflies in full uniform ran security.

Catwalks branch off into the Upper Circuit and Lower Circuit. The Upper Circuit skirts along the top of Bosseti Falls and gives a top down view of the cataratas. Here, the water is more orderly. It queues and marches forward in step without fatigue or complaint rather than the jailbreak rioting earlier. However, after falling nearly a football field in length, the finale is no less a meat grinder. Uncountable fingers of water string out across the horizon. Although the Bosseti's lack the fearsome anger of the Devil's Throat, they are no less awesome in their majesty.

A flock of seven budgies on growth hormones, colored with retina-burning lime green and bright red, circled towards the falls twice. From my vantage, they appeared suicidal, but somewhere in their view was a landing pad. On the third approach, six disappeared into the falls. The seventh, and smallest, tried following in but had to abort and power up as the deck crew cleared a space. Two failed attempts to set down finally succeeded on the third.

The Lower Circuit requires climbing steps, occasionally a few slippery ones. These catwalks arrive at the base of Bosseti Falls, also Ramirez Falls, and a boat launch. Various tours are available by speedboats that take you and your Canon for the most spectacular views, even up the gut to laugh in the face of El Diablo. How close depends on water volumes. Landlubbers can knock the Tropic of Capricorn's heat off by following one branch of catwalk directly into the spray of a huge catarata for a fun dousing.

Does Your Meter Work?!

A trip to the Argentine side of Iguacu Falls takes a full day. The Devil burns two hours, and the Upper and Lower Circuits consume an hour and a half each. Tack on the visitor center, rest, snacks, and your own private time to gaze at this marvelous wonder.

The Brazilian side takes a couple of hours. It offers an opposite field angle of the Devil's Throat, and the chance to get soaked by some of Satan's cataratas. Aracnophiles can see a commonwealth of huge spiders sun tanning as they net-fish for lunch. Long snouted raccoons tamely hang out among the crowd. One adult smelled food, and pulled a bag out of a lady's hands, only to turn up its anteater nose at her baby's food.

Iguacu Falls is a highlight-reel destination in South America. Whether you stay in Puerto Iguacu in Argentina or Foz do Iguacu in Brazil (where it's cheaper) and only border hop for the day in order to take in both sides, then customs formalities are minimal. Or there's a Sheraton on the Argentine side with dashing views.

At vernal Iguacu National Park, the valves are wide open in a staggering demonstration of Nature's force. By mingling with her children as they live in eco-harmony, you'll understand better why people's passions get raised over her rainforests. You'll see this, and much more. Hopefully no jaguars.

BAHIA BONITA CLUB

There was a time when Rio de Janeiro's splendor was unknown; all those spectacular beaches were just empty stretches of gorgeous sand wondering when someone was going to brain up and start building hotels and restaurants. Whoever took the first step had the right idea, and the rest is history. As they say, any success began as a few sketches on someone's kitchen table.

North of Rio approximately 600 miles lies Transcoso, a town that three Argentinean amigos, Fredy, a salesman, Nico, a rubber products manufacturer, and Ricardo, a pension owner, discovered while on holiday. They found the cobalt Atlantic licking mile upon mile of freckled quartzy sand, and not a lot more. There were a few decent places to stay in the sleepy village twenty minutes away by foot, but the majority of accommodations were budget *pousadas*. The only choices on the beach were four walls and something resembling a bed.

Two architects were hired, and this coterie of would-be hoteliers began to scheme and dream during the Southern Hemisphere's 2001 summer. The work began, and now, the modernistic Bahia Bonita Club has opened. Its initial phase is a fourplex hewn of eucalyptus logs and finished with angelina pedra, vinhatico, and tatajuba woods.

Two suites, the upper Sea Room and lower Sand Room, face the ocean, about 30 seconds away. A mammoth cashew tree altruistically shades the other two suites facing opposite, Forest and Sky. Beyond the nuts lies the Rio Verde River, more a stream than a torrent, and further beyond, rocky outcrops protrude from a canopy of broadleaf jungle.

Bahia Bonita Club is built on the Discovery Coast, an ecological reserve nominated as a World Heritage Site. These Bahian rainforests are considered the worlds richest in terms of the number of species of trees per acre. To save them, only 5% of the land is permitted for development, and the Bohia Bonita Club is in. The Club uses solar energy where it can; their policy is no air-conditioning, phones, TV, or e-mail. In throaty, broken English, Nico says "We want customers who appreciate nature, and like to live with nature, so we designed Bahia Bonita just like nature. We are not artists, but we love art, and nature."

Decor of the rooms is simple. A double and single bed, twin showerheads, a separate lavatory, a bar/sitting area, and a hammock on the balcony. The ceilings' open-air and sloping lines are designed to funnel in the Atlantic Easterlies and splash cool air from top down, keeping each room fresh and mosquito-free.

A simple, solid menu of pastas, steaks, and seafood range in price from 10-18 reals. Sandwiches and desserts cost 5-6. ($1=2.4 reals)

To attract the beautiful bodies, this year, the Club has a pair of lovely common areas and a small weight center. Next year, you'll find paragliding, kayaks, snorkeling, sailing, and horses.

For reservations, e-mail bahiabonita@hotmail.com, cell (55) (73) 668 1565 (ask for the Sea Room). They'll meet you at Porto Seguro's airport and show you to your new home for free. For the intrepid traveler, take the ferry crossing at Porto Seguro, and then hop a Transcoso bus. Ask for the praia, which is "beach" in Brazilian Portuguese. It's pronounced like "prior" with a British accent. Once at the sand, turn right, or south, and ask for "Praia Nudissmo", or Nude Beach, which isn't unless you want it to be, at your desire and participation. With an Empty Quarter's stretch of sand such as that at Transcoso Beach, you'll find privacy somewhere.

VIAGRA? ANTLER VELVET? NAH, GIMME THE GLOBE

Why is it that two people see the same movie, and one viewer can't contain his enthusiasm while the other finds the whole thing a replacement for Sominex without side effects? To one gourmet, turnips are the best thing since sun dried tomatoes, and another dinner guest would sooner dine with Idi Amin. Why are one traveler's senses on overload while the grump in the next seat can't wait to get out of town? The world's destinations are an endless list of globe, or "G" Spots. Something exceptional about their offerings pushes your buttons, flies your kite, floats your boat. The following is my personal unfinished list of the world's G-Spots. Feel free to snort your disagreement, and create your own list of places that tickle your world.

ANGKOR WAT. Angkor Wat, in war torn Cambodia, is not one spot but the generic name used for a collection of fortresses, temples, and structures built during the height of the Khmer civilization that spanned from approximately 800 until 1200 AD. The Khmer ruled most of the region, including present-day Laos, Vietnam, Thailand, and even parts of China. The three main sites and sights they left behind are called Angkor Wat, Angkor Thom, and Ta Prohm. Angkor Wat (Angkor is from the Sanskrit word *nagara* which means *city*. *Vot* is Cambodian for *pagoda* or *Buddhist shrine*) is first surrounded by a moat more than four miles long with a quarter mile walkway over the moat and through a splendid portico of columns supporting a roof; it's like an enormous stone tunneled fence. The walk leads up to the entrance which has huge blocks, comprised mainly of sandstone and also some limonite, fitted together without cement, and as straight and true as the horizon that welds the Cambodian sky and sea.

The brilliant and delicate carvings, thousands and thousands of characters, meticulously carved in bas-relief on a surrounding perimeter wall totaling more than 17,000 square feet. Delicately whittled in precise, minute detail, the carvings dedicate legends to war and gods. From a network of hallways that shape the center, five majestic towers rise conically like enormous rock asparagus tips. Angkor Wat is best seen at sundown when the sun aims its focused rays and gives the edifice a sacred, incandescent glow amid the darkening natural surroundings.

A stone fence nearly two miles square with five gates of entry encloses Angkor Thom (Thom is from Thai *thom = great*, and the effect is indeed one of incredible size and ornate complexity). The centerpiece, *The Bayon*, is ablaze with faces. The haunting visage of Brahma sculpted on each side of 20 extraordinary quadruply sided towers soar all around. Moss and lichen add greenish-black hues to the washed white stone. Early Khmers venerated Brahma, the creator god of the Hindu religion, before allegiances eventually moved to Buddha. The religious clarity of vision is mated to a generally clean landscaped setting.

Popular Ta Prohm, on the other hand, hasn't been cleaned up. Much of this edifice lies in rubble, yet an amazing amount still stands. The site demonstrates the phenomenal power of the jungle where elephantine trees have grown over walls and pushed through stone. In breathtaking dimensions, roots wider than telephone poles wrap themselves around structures like boa constrictors on their prey. A tree grows from the top of a building or fence and its roots tentacle down agonizingly, slowly swallowing its victim.

The viewer from the West feels overwhelmed, as when seeing the Egyptian Pyramids. In each place, one is puzzled by the simplest of questions: how an ancient culture could conceive of moving, and carving, the sheer amount and size of stone, and raising the works to such heights and symmetries. This is the architecture of genius combined with the organizational ability of brilliant rulers. In contrast to the damning evidence of the Khmer Rouge's madness, revealed in Phnom Penh, Angkor Wat takes us to the precisely opposite level on the scale of astonishing human creations. Cambodia pulls in two directions: to celebrate mankind for its incredible abilities, and loathe it for its shocking primitiveness.

My sacred place is not expensive. Siem Riep, ten miles from Angkor Wat complex, can be reached by plane or speedboat from Phnom Penh. Guesthouses for as little as $3 line the streets.

CHRISTCHURCH. Think of England without the decay, not England today and not London ever, just English country towns in the 1950's. Don't hesitate about landing in New Zealand's *Garden City* where every house, every yard, everywhere flashes flowers, shrubs, and trees. Weeping willows, like huge, green, beehive haircuts, follow the rivers and canals meandering through downtown, along golf courses, and among parks. Perfect roses and blood red carnations linger below enormous oak trees. The city center Botanic Garden beside Christ's College, an exclusive boys school, fills every horticultural fancy.

Swim and surf in nearby Sumner and tan the day away after some dicey driving to Taylor's Mistake. The Wizard inhabits the centerpiece of ChCh, Cathedral Square. Witty, stand-up philosophy from his *Speaker's Corner on a Road Trip* is yours to enjoy or mock gently amid the downtown business area and Cashel Street, an outdoor pedestrian mall. Superb food is everywhere. Sumner has *The Ruptured Duck* for pizza, *Zollie's* on Selwyn Street serves the best Ploughman's Lunch this side of Birmingham, *The Dux Deluxe*, just down from The Cathedral, washes back the day's comestibles. Particular folks should try the unheard-of but often delightful New Zealand wines available. For sure, try *Harrington's* spirits. John Harrington tilts his head and confesses, "We have great water here." What ties together the elements of Christchurch's tapestry of attractions is the spirit of its people. Smiles and hellos are as abundant as the flora. The Park Hotel is the poshest place in town, and no shortage of "backpackers" or hostels means Christchurch offers an easy access to all ranges of accommodation. A trip to Christchurch is Good On Ya, especially if you head to the NZ Alps afterward, zip to Kaikoura on the east coast for a day of whale watching, hike northward, or fly off to Fiji or Tahiti.

NEW YORK. To include the big town, the biggest town going if you count variety rather than voting population, is to admit that life is more than clean sidewalks and flowering lanes. Most striking of all that is arresting about New York is its almost scary sense of absolute personal freedom, bordering on anarchy. You can be or imitate or make fun of anyone or anything you want, but you're on your own. And to make it in New York on New Yorkers' terms, everybody knows, every visitor senses in five minutes, only the best will do. New York represents the greatest and the worst that

America has to offer, and the rest of us can envy or fear, abide, or stomach. Every thing else rests between. One moment on the streets of Manhattan is a revelation why so many songs are sung, poems written, and stories told about The Big Apple. And that it was no accident that terrorists would want to focus their angst against America through NY.

Scary places remain, none more than Ground Zero, but even with its two front teeth knocked out, the kinder and gentler streets that tourists and decent folks walk have been reclaimed by the people. Cops are everywhere, musicians and sidewalk painters fill Times Square again, and the subways now move residents, not criminal armies. Equally engrossing as the sights are the sounds. Some of the best entertainment the city produces are the snippets of other's conversations as they pass by. With open ears eavesdropping for "Apple Bites", if forced to choose between sight or sound while in town, you'd be hard pressed to decide. The corner of Macdougal and Bleecker in Greenwich Village is one of the most exciting street corners on Earth. Its eclectic shops and singularly distinctive settings could only be New York. The Y's are not as benign as the ones at home, and the dorms rarely have rooms to let. Housing is apartmenting, so bed and breakfasts come without shrubs (except on rooftops in Star Trek-dimensioned garden plots) and at high tariffs. Reserve in advance, for accommodation is always tight in NY. Best of all, stay with a pal or find a long-lost relative. There is no better guide to bagels and byways than a real Noo Yawker. As a friend said during a cold beer in steamy Saigon one night, "If you're bored in New York, check for a pulse."

SAIGON. Sorry, I can't call it by its latest colonial name, Ho Chi Minh City. Saigon, a frantic case half being born and half lying in triage, is the most severe, enchanting, acute big Asian city. Her seductive spell attaches the superlative - affix the label "the most," "the best," "the worst" then proceed at your own risk. Saigon is the dirtiest, the raunchiest, the friendliest, the dodgiest, the most fun, the most crooked, the most intriguing. Saigon has the most hectic streets, the most complicated layered society, the most beautiful women, the most potential, the most colorful past, the nicest scenery, the hardest working people, the dumbest behavior, the best sights.

Vietnam cooks up and serves the best value for money and, give or take a few memorable dishes in Indonesia and elsewhere, the best food in South-East Asia. In the center of Saigon, two magnificent reminders of French colonization, a Catholic Cathedral and the Post Office temper Hand Job Park's nighttime shameless vulgarity (yes, it's earned that name, and just why you think it did, or fear it might have). On the other side of the park is the Presidential Palace. Just down the street is the former American Embassy. Brand-new glass office towers sit mostly empty, waiting for the world's movers and shakers to arrive with suitcases of plans and cash and intrigue.

Vietnam's Indo-China cousins, Cambodia and Laos, have populations of no more than five or six million, yet Vietnam is close to 80 million. What is it about this puzzling country that galvanizes action, activity, happenings, be they good or bad? Why did the fireworks of the 60's go off here and not in Indonesia who was having similar communist threats? Or some other country? I don't know if I'm in love with Saigon or hate its guts.

The New World Hotel tops the heap and Pham Ngu Lao Street overflows with cheapies from five to twelve dollars. Mid-range hotels, lead by the prime-located Rex, fill city center.

PHUKET. The word that immediately came to mind to describe the blanket kissing my soles was *plush*. Then came *pure*. My feet had never touched something so exquisite. The unsullied, virtuous sand squeaks against your skin while forming a footprint! The simple sensation was a revelation, instantaneously explaining the huge development on the southwest coast of Thailand. Beach huts and up mingle among Club Med and an assortment of five-star resorts. Waikiki-like Patong Beach has many more choices of hotels, restaurants, shops, and clubs than quieter Koron Beach, a 15 minute drive over headland separating the two waterfront treasures. What's to do? How about scuba diving, parasailing, water skiing, jet-skiing, sailing, windsurfing, shooting ranges, go-carts, miniature golf, elephant rides, sunbathing, sunbather watching, etc. And loads of nightlife. Phuket's (pronounced POO-

Does Your Meter Work?!

KET) hedonism has something for everyone. Thailand has its warts, but Phuket is a clean and decent breeze.

QUEBEC CITY. It's only a surprise choice until you've been. My first time in Quebec City, a world heritage site, I stepped off the bus in front of the Chateau Frontenac and went short of breath. The patriarchal hotel towers pre-eminently, grand and proud like the French who gave it life. In behind, I tingled looking down the stairs from the top of Place Royale. A stroll up La Grande Allée among the restaurants and shops is a time machine circa the French Revolution. The Citadel and the Plains of Abraham, where General Wolfe defeated General Montcalm to gain control for England, is Canada's most interesting history spot. Those lucky enough to see a hockey game before Les Nordiques left town witnessed the single minded passion and love the French carry for their heroes, and their language, their culture, which is and isn't ours in the rest of North America. They howled disapprovingly at the referee for not penalizing the visiting side even when no infraction occurred, and snickered like kids when a Nordique escaped with the obvious. There's no such thing as too much of Quebec City. Le Ville de Quebec is well set up for all levels of touring, from the backpacker and hitchhiker to the family needing the proper accommodations.

EDINBURGH. The soot plastered to the stone buildings was the exact image of England I arrived in the UK to see. Don't run me through, Scotty, I know you're not English, any more than your noble history is English, and I have no intention of labeling you thus. Scotland's fiercely independent stance is part of the conjoining warmth Edinburgh oozes to visitors in its pubs, lunch spots, and shops. The North Sea's wind provokes a perpetually runny nose and a chill up your kilt, but briskness only applies to the weather, not the friendliness of Edinburgh denizens. Narrow alleys and stone construction, blackened from the chimneys spewing coal dust, lack architectural splendor, yet calmness in the streets, and a days meander within the walls of the castle keeping watch over the city rates Edinburgh a G-Spot rating for titillating the jaded traveler's remaining senses. B&B's are your best bet for getting started, outside of the pubs, of course. Meet a Scot and learn why you're not in England.

Does Your Meter Work?!

VIENNA. Another platitude? Europe is replete with magnificent cities that to exclude any is a disservice and therefore an incomplete list. However, everyone's G-Spot list of world stops is unique, and Vienna rattled my cage for reasons beyond her obvious allures. A deliciously memorable lunch facing the Opera House was a good start. The University of Vienna, the Schönbrunn Palace, and Vienna's musical legacy adds to her enticements. Most appealing is an intangible commodity, the Viennese deportment. They walk like Austrian soldiers from two centuries past, as if, even at noon, they have somewhere to go and something to do when they get there, and they will get there soon, danke. The world has two kinds of people - those that have been to Vienna, and those yet to go and discover fine cakes, fine schnapps, amazing music, and sparkling museums, all aglow with the glitter of pre-WW1 Europe. Nowhere else is remotely Viennese. When you go, take schillings. Even dorm rooms cost lots, and the schnapps and pastries need tasting to authenticate that your senses are alive after all.

JASPER. Within the Canadian Rockies, the earthier sibling of glam Banff asks its visitors for one thing - to just be alive and there. Jasper is not Banff, which dares you to find open spaces and escape the car exhausts and the tourist flocks. Here pristine air *wants* to be inhaled and exhaled. Crystal clear aquamarine-green-turquoise-azure water (no word quite covers the color) loafs in the lakes or roars down the regal mountains. After a rain, the operative word is clean: the whole place looks old and renewed, as though taste was natural and not learned. Elk, easily one of the world's cagiest and skittish creatures, stroll in herds down Main Street or graze on residents' lawns -- and probably on your hotel's shrubbery, too. Fishing for rainbow and brook trout in nearby Maligne Lake is one of Mother Nature's most rewarding outdoor adventures. My first time skiing was at Marmot Basin. I never learned to like the actual skiing part of a ski trip, only everything else, like the mountains, the snow, the lodges, the hot tubs, the beverages....

Getting to Jasper is not so simple as getting to Vienna or New York, however. First you fly to Edmonton and rent a car or take the train. The lovely and well-appointed Jasper Park Lodge is first class all the way but there are reasonable hotels and motels, and even rustic cabins (complete with deer, too). Many homes in town rent rooms, and there are cliffside hostels to rough it in.

HONORABLE G-SPOT HONORABLE MENTIONS. Berlin, Kathmandu, Kandy (Sri Lanka), The entire French Riviera, Santorini (Greece), Rome, Borneo, Hong Kong's living skyline.

FUTURE G-SPOTS. The world is too big to have seen it all, however through research, recon, intelligence gathering, and being a bug on the wall, G-Spots I vow to caress and soon are Cape Town, Prague, Istanbul, Santiago, Beirut, all of Israel, a free Burma (can't promise the soon part), Monterey, Stockholm, St. Petersburg, Morocco. But those are for my senses. Touch your memories to discover the G-Spots in your past. Trust me, it's pure pleasure to do so, at least in your imagination.

CA$H IN ON YOUR LUCK BY TEACHING ENGLISH <u>OVERSEAS.</u>

So you want to teach English as a second language (ESL) overseas? You want to walk through the doors and peek over the walls of exotic lands to learn mysterious secrets while doing it? Good idea! English has evolved into the universal language, and teaching it has become an effective and available vehicle to work around the globe without studying a craft for a lifetime, or persisting at a job for years until your abilities and experience make you a valuable enough commodity to be paid for what you know. Globalization has created more and more fledgling democracies, which in turn have created work in nearly any big, non-English speaking city in the world. The most popular region in the last couple of decades has been Asia, with Japan in the vanguard. Economic prosperity made Korea and Taiwan equally accessible and rewarding, but they are less well known here in North America. Lately Eastern Europe and Latin America have developed into solid markets.

Taiwan always has a huge shortage of teachers. I taught there for eight months, saved $11,000, then took off traveling. I took in the cock-fights in the Philippines, scuba dove in the South China Sea, climbed the tallest peak in South East Asia, hitchhiked from Brunei to Bangkok, emotionally swayed between the ghastly evidence of the Khmer Rouge and the ineluctable Angkor Wat in Cambodia, then stopped in Saigon for another teaching stint. I arrived in the evening, and had a job the next afternoon. After Vietnam, there was white-water rafting in the Himalayas, Hindu blessings at sunrise on The Ganges River, and the Indian train system, until my tanks were finally empty in Sri Lanka. When my plane touched down in North America two years later, I still had $7,200! Is it only teaching English per se that allows such adventures? Of course not, but for someone who isn't a "something" i.e. nurse, chef, computer person, there's nothing else that offers the freedom or earning power.

Wherever you want to go, anytime is a good time. Regions differ in their best times. Major holidays close schools and distract students from studying. In Asia, between Christmas and the Lunar

New Year, the job market weakens, and from the New Year until three weeks post it is useless.

Having a degree, previous experience, Teaching English as a Second Language (TESL) certification, or speaking the native language of the country are advantages, but they are NOT essential if you want to profit from your native English speaking ability. If you have none of the previous qualities, then instead of 1000 jobs available to you, that number plummets to 980. Because of The United Status's influence, American and Canadian accents receive better favor than any other i.e. British, New Zealand etc.

Before setting out a little groundwork is necessary. The most important hurdle to overcome is to stop thinking like an American. Living in Asia, for example, is not akin to renting an apartment in San Francisco's Chinatown for a while. It's Asia, it's The Show, a different planet unto itself. The soundest preparation is to ready your mind for a tidal wave of new information to interpret. Decisions on length of stay, hours of work per week, working to save money or to party or to study etc. are important points to consider, however these plans are most difficult to formulate stateside because the destination WILL be much different than your mind's eye can suppose. Unless your schedule is set in concrete, surrender to time and a period of information gathering once overseas to sort out the future.

Fearing to venture abroad without the so-called safety net of an already arranged job and a greeting party at the airport is a perfect example of thinking like an American. The situation boils down to, "Do you wait for someone to bring you flowers or do you plant your own garden?" With this thought in mind, be aware that few schools recruit from abroad. Those that do, or must, are probably a pain to work for and as a result they probably cannot enlist enough teachers from those already in country. Or they are located in a hinterland.

Arriving independently ensures the freedom from commitment should your eventual employer fail to be citizen of the year. It's a long way from home to feel caught under another's thumb. Well, what did you expect? There's no such thing as a free lunch; the cost of airplane tickets and other recruitment perks have been calculated somewhere along the line. Schools are private businesses, and subject to the universal rules of commerce. But getting fully prepared requires a little inside information.

A call to an embassy to investigate a particular country's work scene will be met with official, bureaucratic requirements, for example, a letter from an employer guaranteeing employment. Ninety-nine and forty-four one hundredths percent of teachers obtained their jobs by skirting the red tape and entering the country as tourists. They then either arranged work permits or went at it under the table. Do not let this strange, underhanded sounding advice scare you off. It's simply one, albeit a crucial one, of the hoops to jump through. The authorities know where the schools and employment agents preside, and they could raid and deport every teacher in a matter of hours if desired. The unspoken truth is that teachers are wanted and needed.

Another hoop, and a cost of doing business, is the necessary visa run. Exiting a country with little or no baggage then returning later that night as a tourist would alert even the most witless customs official. By never admitting that work is the intention behind a visit, everyone is allowed to play the game.

What should you take? Don't take more than one bag. Dress codes are fairly relaxed and wherever you go will have no shortage of shopping. Expensive, chic clothing suffers an unnecessary beating. If you have a degree or other certificates, take an original. Toiletries and prescriptions are widely available. If you have extra eyewear, take them.

Most work is in developing or undeveloped countries. As a middle class emerges, and upper class students spend their new toy called money, your list of students becomes a Who's Who of the city. The generosity of many is astonishing. Sources of work are divided under two headings: in a classroom at a school (the majority of this work is with kids), and "privates," typically with adults. In the former's case, grinning, fawning parents seek out their child's foreign instructor anticipating to hear gushing praise for their kid's abilities, and to pinch a free conversation quickie for themselves. Private students hire a teacher because they have time and sufficient wealth. So often, this class of student consists of business owners or their wives.

Finding work is the easiest part of the process. Various avenues include the classifieds of any local English publication, agents and agencies, word-of-mouth, bulletin boards in hostels and universities, and in the unlikeliest places. If you are likeable, an amazing quantity of business surfaces. Students suddenly have a cousin or friend in the market for a teacher. During an interview, if ANY red flags raise, walk away. You hold all the cards.

Wages vary from country to school to student. In Asia, realistically it's up to $40 per hour. Japan pays better because of the cost of living, Taiwan is around $20 while Vietnam's rate is $8-$11, Cambodia $6, Nepal around $2. Struggling countries in South America and Africa range from work for room and/or board to market rates in the thriving big cities. Europe fluctuates from high single digits to mid twenties. Schools pay less than privates per hour, but are not wracked with cancellations.

Lesson plans? Staff meetings? Supervision? To be pedantic is the kiss of death. A better title than teacher is "English Language Consultant." One-to-one teaching is conversation, articulation, and pronunciation practice for the student. At first, improvement comes quickly for one of two reasons: from dusting off their rusty skills or from discovering an ability that had lain dormant from timidity. In a classroom setting, generally the administration hands over a "connect the dots" textbook and says, "Room 3 upstairs." The key, particularly with adults, is to charm and amuse. If the students report favorably, then hours, and paydays, increase.

You may not always feel charmed. To pull their people out of poverty, the English-needing countries have sacrificed environmental needs. A blue haze fills the air, the water is impotable, rats and cockroaches are a part of the scenery, dogs bark all over the streets, from both ends if you catch my drift. Riding in vehicles is a game of Russian Roulette. The good, such as your students, is so good, but the bad can be brutal. As a result, much of your time fluctuates between utter contentment, and utter contempt. You will have bad moments, bad days, even bad weeks. There is no point in trying to sugarcoat the downside of being so far away from what is familiar and comfortable. Remember three things:

1. It's not forever (unless you want it to be).
2. Your learning curve has never been steeper.

3. There is a price to pay for everything.

The desire to teach English abroad must spark from within; it's something that you really want to do, and something that you're prepared to make happen for yourself. If you're of the mind: "Well, I could sell shoes at the mall, or cut grass for my uncle, or go overseas and teach English," then cut grass in your newly discounted shoes, as your life on the other side of the ditch would be hell. As well, if you only like vanilla, think hard if you're up to the challenge.

Don't go until your heart is absolutely ready. Once ready, jump in with both feet! Only look forward. After the jet lag wears off and your new life establishes itself, it's clear how simple the entire process is.

Being born a native English speaker is equivalent to winning a lottery before you've bought a ticket. You carry, without lifting a finger, a portable skill that millions kill themselves to gain and for some, quite literally, their lives depend upon getting. Although venturing to another country to work is a big dare, see it as an extraordinary opportunity, with the broadest definition of extraordinary. In time, after your traveling afar is over, and you have suddenly found yourself back on home turf, you'll miss the new worlds you discovered, even when you conclude that your unremarkable little hometown is one of the world's best-kept secrets.

MEXICO ALL INCLUSIVE
To Sloth or not to Sloth

What's the one thing you have lots of when staying at an all-inclusive holiday resort in Puerto Vallarta, Mexico? The answer is *everything*.

Food? In buffet style, breakfast gets sprawled out starting, apparently, around 7. At 10:30 or so, they clear that away and begin gearing up for lunch. A stroll cases out the menu. The soup station seems like a good place to start, but wait, that friendly guy who served the toothsome leg of beef at dinner the night before has something steaming away out the other side. He's nicely set up next to the five choices of dessert. By the time his fresh ham is evident, last night's main course is now today's soup. Wonderful. Efficient.

Forget the soup. What else is out today? The bread racks are stocked, and stacked, with baguettes, croissants, buns, and loaves. Two banks of four steam tables serve an array of fresh vegetables, potatoes, rice, chicken, and on and on. Now, a decision is required. How much of which item to take in order to find a balance between sampling enough fare to satisfy your curiosity, and trying to walk to the beach without calling in a mobile crane.

Repeats of dishes were rare during my week of immoderation, a double-edged sword because great cuisine should be enjoyed again, but what else could the chef have under his bonnet?

The service is perfect, as far from that at home as you can get. Restaurant staff hustle like rookies clearing, pouring, wiping, and dodging kids. The bottom of your coffee cup or wine glass is feared as though it hid the Loch Ness Monster. Fill, refill, refill. Pee, get refilled.

Time for this brat to come clean. One evening at dinner, the grillman serving beef chop suey skipped over to the marinated pork chops and onion station to deliver something. He was gone close to 15 seconds. Somehow I withstood the wait, plate in hand and dying to be served. I was so spoiled, that if this wayward warden hadn't rebounded in haste, I was on the verge of bolting,

163

quick as a cadaver, over to the fresh pasta with two kinds of sauce and perfectly grated Parmesan.

Between grazing, this hotel presented four bars, opening at 10 and closing, in theory, 16 hours later. Standing in the way of a Dirty Monkey, a Banana Mama, wine, beer, or any highball you'd care for is your refusal to ask.

Sports? Tennis lessons at 9, for an hour. The archery center opens as the nets on the two ping-pong tables go up. The water sports shed has boogie boards, kayaks, windsurfing, and sailing - lessons provided. The peanut-shaped pool, surrounded by reclining beach beds, hosts water polo, pool volleyball, musical swimming chairs, and tequila volleyball (use your imagination). There's shuffleboard, beach volleyball, dance lessons, horseshoe pits, badminton courts, bocce ball areas, and a steroidal teenager's delight, a weight room. If gym's not your bag, or you hate spilling your drink during an activity, there's bingo, guacamole class, bartending class, language class, art class.

Decision making and strategic planning still too hard on the head? The beach is a no-brainer. Middle-aged spreads on bodies of both sexes outweigh other body types, still there's everything from slight and tight to droopy and dodgy. Swimsuits? Bikinis fabricated from dental floss. Bronzed beefcakes strutting like peacocks after the hens, and everyone's favorite beach victim, the alabaster lobster suffering from the sun that some just can't seem to let go. A willowy thirtysomething lady saunters by, clad in her string bikini, a cell phone hanging from her hip. Treasure of the Sierra Madres. Oops, wrong country.

Even in this parade of free entertainment and armies of entertainers, a few activities inevitably cost extra. The eyes of the parasailing guys go ka-ching as sun-soaked flyers meet up with the birds on a 15-minute high-altitude spin around the bay. These safe, undemanding, infectious rides have the folks of every age paying around $25, and just as the sun never set on the British Empire, the parachute never seemed to set onto the sand. Each person would plop down in practically the same footprints, and the next harnessed-up customer clicked in and the boat powered up again and again.

Forget daisy chain paraflops, I wanted scuba diving. A little shopping around destroyed any illusions about Mexico still coming cheap. Seventy-eight dollars was the most reasonable trip. The other option was to go tanned toe to tanned toe with the Time Share tyrants. Their offices offered gifts for the right to listen to their pitch. I faked interest and took the plunge. Ninety minutes of my time earned scuba diving for two. But the price also included more than I had bargained for.

An icebreaker conversation, lunch, and a tour of the impressive grounds and apartments led to the Closing Room.

"If you like the terms, we have what we call FVI, or First Visit Incentive (compliant with Mexican law as they had already painfully pointed out) meaning you get the one-bedroom suite *plus* the studio room for US$42,000, then a $329 annual maintenance fee. This assures you one week per year, 50% more fee getting you into your place at Christmas, New Year's, or Easter."

I had the stock cheap guy's response all prepared, and they looked at me as if they were ready for baloney, so I delivered: "I can't give you a commitment of that size right now. I'm the point guy with my family. I'm supposed to get information and talk about it at dinner. Can I take the numbers with me?"

"We understand, but the answer, I'm afraid, is no, we have to turn them in. I was hoping you could keep them clear in your mind."

Time for the cheapie retreat and regroup: "No I'm not signing and committing anything this fast."

Up come the reinforcements: Somehow Manager #1 arrived just on cue. He was debriefed on my unique intellect and amiability.

"So your family is out looking at other time shares, then you'll compare tonight, that's it, right?"

Time for a segue or deflection or bigger fib: "Nope, I left them shopping."

Rebuttal: "That doesn't seem fair."

Battle fatigue: "What doesn't seem fair?"

Shock troops called up: "That you have to be here and they're off vacationing."

Back to the bunker mentality: "No big deal."

Pregnant pause.

Interrogation of the POW: "So your family sent you?"

Name, rank, and serial number: "I sent myself for all of us."

Good interrogator role: "Do they trust your judgment?"

John Wayne prisoner of war monosyllable response: "Sure."

Sneaky enemy officer trap springs: "So why wouldn't they trust you to make this decision?"

Duke punch to the enemy nose: "Because it ain't gonna happen right here, right now."

Victory, music up, popcorn bags on the floor. He departed silently. Wait. The second interrogator, bad cop. My pitchman waved Manager #2 over.

"This is Jim, he said there's six in his family, I don't know…"

I heard words and phrases like equity, convenience, what's best for me, prime carrying charges, and on and on until my cranium was out of RAM. He gave way. After a decade or an hour, I was alone, rewarded, scuba laden at last.

No.

Up rose interrogator #3. A woman this time, the ultimate dirty-trick weapon for a single guy, a woman of such beauty and clear of eye that Satan had to have broken the mold, and she took one last crack at capturing the whole battalion. I was Odysseus resisting the Siren's offensive, with the single-minded focus of the scuba prize battling her allures.

When she finally surrendered, I fled unescorted to the in-house travel agency who booked the scuba for the next day. Odysseus survived the voyage, except in our own little Greek tragedy, the underwater view during the dive was reduced to a few yards from rain and cloud.

If you have the money for an all-inclusive, go! Advocating this style of holiday is easy since at times in every breast hedonism rides up front. There's going to be a ton to do, and with all the food and drink offerings, the kid-in-the-candy-store syndrome will be in command at the beginning. After a few days, sensibilities return, and your indulgences will become more evenhanded. We became part of the scene, more inhabitants than hungry tourists. We drank the water, learned a little Spanish, and played at being free, free, free at last with more of everything than we would ever use up.

CHINESE PAPER CUTS

Nearly 2,000 years ago, the Chinese began making patterns out of delicate rice paper to transfer embroidery patterns. As the patterns became more intricate, people began to appreciate the intrinsic beauty of the paper cuts themselves, and the craft evolved into a folk art in its own right. The drier climate of Hu Bei province in the north especially lent itself to the art and it became known as the home of Chinese Paper Cuts.

Subject matter is often taken from Chinese opera. The art also relies on a number of symbols — Chi-lin, for example, is a mystical animal thought to bring children. Peach, pine, and cranes suggested longevity. Dragons, lions, and tigers symbolized courage and strength. Serpents were the villains representing cunning and evil powers of supernatural origin.

Writings from the T'ang (618-907) and Sung (960-1127) dynasties indicate that part of any girl's preparation for marriage included training in paper cutting, as well as embroidery. At funerals, cut paper symbols were used extensively. Along with paper shoes and clothing, messages and symbols might be made and burnt as gifts to accompany the dead in the other life.

Paper cutting came to Europe via Middle Eastern and Turkish trade routes. Paper, a rare commodity, was mostly found in monasteries where monks incorporated paper cutting into their illuminated manuscripts.

Today, both men and women create Chinese paper cuts only for decoration. Chinese paper cuts are cut from compacted paper blocks, as many as 50 at a time, then peeled off and hand colored, or the whole bundle can be colored at once. Dyes applied to the top layer quickly soak down. Although traditionalists prefer to continue crafting them by hand, technology makes the life of an artisan much easier.

The craft has changed and grown into many different levels and forms; from the simple snowflakes of elementary art class, to masterpieces sold at high values. The paper cuts shown are from Hu Bei province. If you want some of your own, they're inexpensive, and found easily in the West in Chinese markets or commercial areas.

For an excellent overview of Chinese paper cuts from all regions of China, go to www.seu.edu.cn/art/english/enga4.htm#art128, or search "Chinese Paper Cuts" on Google.com.

A LAKE OF GOLD AT THE END OF A RAINBOW

"So how's your daughter doin' in school?" I asked my fishing partner Preston sitting at the other end of the boat.

"Ah, she's never any problem."

"It's great when your kids....

WWWWWWOOOOOOWWWWWW!! My fly rod curled over like a hyperactive question mark.

"I got one!" I screeched.

"Nah, you've snagged a rock," tried my skipper.

"Forget th..."

Then it launched three feet, waggled twice, and splashed down. Our eyeballs popped out, bounced against themselves, and somehow found their way back into their sockets. With the incarnation of the "rock" confirmed, the sing of my reel announced the spirit that this trout carried.

"BIG RAINBOW!" Preston declared.

ZZZZZZZZZZZZZZZZ spun my spool, evaporating the remainder of the 150 feet of sinking line before moving on to the cloth backing. I gripped the rod in my left hand, high above the handle for leverage, and palmed the free-wheeling reel with my right, a manual drag to prevent this prize from getting too far for free.

It ran, then paused for a breather. My right hand rewound as fast as it could twirl until the fish lost patience. It made another break for liberty, fleeing until its anaerobic energy depleted again.

"Whirl now that you have the chance!" I ordered myself.

Without maintaining a taut line, and my rod tip up, the trout could spit the hook out while resting. Hooks famously tear through their tender mouths, but this guy had bit hard.

"We gotta 50/50 chance of landing this guy!" squealed my sidekick. "Keep him snug!"

My prisoner jarred the rod again, forcing my left grip to reclench, and I let it run with about 25% resistance. It was so strong and angry, too much brake would snap the tapered leader, ample where knotted to the 20 pound sinking line, but thread-like at the hook.

ZZZZZ tighten. ZZZZZ tighten. ZZZZZ tighten. Back and forth the tug-of-war swung. Lunges and plunges. Bounds and belly flops. Blast-offs and re-entries. Detonations and dives. Right to left it took us on the ride of both of our lives. ZZZZZ tighten. ZZZZZ tighten.

Then, no ZZZZZ. Its silver flashed along the surface as it seemed to charge the boat, either disoriented or somehow crossbred with a grizzly. It stopped and floated where we could see there was lots of it, in case there was still any question. My reeling drew the line tense. Infuriated by the pull, it dove under the 12 foot aluminum craft and out the other side.

ZZZZZ tighten. ZZZZZ tighten. This brawler was finally running out of steam. The old boy had the pluck left for one last run until finally saying Uncle. Exhausted, it fought the good fight. Preston dipped the net into the crisp mountain water and docked the four and a half pound "Rainbow Warrior."

Close to an hour from the town site of Jasper, Alberta, Maligne (ma-LEEN) Lake nestles into the Canadian Rocky Mountains. It stretches more than 14 miles long, and is only about a mile across, broadening to one and a half at its widest point. Glaciers carved the floor into a V, leaving a depth of 350 feet down the middle.

At an elevation of 5500 feet, the Upper Maligne River feeds into the lake, along with assorted drainage creeks off the mountains. Maligne Lake empties into the Mid Maligne River. Fly-fishing and white-water rafting disrupted the sensitive Harlequin duck breeding grounds, thus permanently closing the river to human use.

The Mid Maligne drops 500 feet of elevation into Medicine Lake, 13.5 miles away. A rockslide from ages past, in conjunction with the undercutting and shoveling actions of a glacier, had blocked the normal outflow of Medicine Lake. As a result, the lake drains through gravel-choked sinkholes through its limestone floor. The water then collects underground to emerge at various spots in the Maligne Canyon some 12 miles away, another 1400 foot descent.

Maligne Lake offers world-class fishing of rainbow and Eastern brook trout. Amid spectacular backdrops of mountains, it opens for the season the third weekend in May, and closes the first weekend of September. There's no ice fishing permitted during winter.

Does Your Meter Work?!

So how did I end up in the Rassle with the Rainbow? We had left Edmonton shortly before midnight the night before, and drove slowly west to Jasper 230 miles away. Then we navigated south, passed the five-star Jasper Park Lodge, climbed the Maligne Lake Road, and pulled into the Maligne Lake parking lot.

4:30 a.m. Mustering a couple of winks in the Chevy Hilton proved a lost cause. Since the sun rises so early in summer, and because the fish stories were getting too thick, it was soon time to put in the boat, rig the electric motor, and doctor the lines.

Egg-sucking leech. I had always thought Preston and I were friends, and I smarted from his insults. I had paid my share of the gas. Then I saw the object of his comment. A fly with black hairs and a fluorescent orange ball imitating a leech that found a fish egg for breakfast was the insider trading for a trout lure. Bait is prohibited.

With the whir of the electric motor pushing the boat about 4 mph, and the haunting call of a loon somewhere in the dawn mist, the depth finder fidgeted between 45 and 185 feet. Far too deep. Trout hang out on the flats and ledges at around 12 feet, so we headed for the lake's far edge.

Fishermen have two choices to propel their boats: electric motors or paddles. The only power boats permitted are double-decker boat tours filled with tourists and warden's speedboats. The tourist vessels create wakes that pitch and toss canoes and 12-foot aluminum boats, so the admirals cut power and troll past. The noise of the engines echoed against the mountains and glaciers, which still engulf whole ridges and faces. Mini-avalanches emitted their roars.

Slowly trolling at the speed a man walks, a stone's throw from shore, we were teased with tugs and pulls, and even landed the odd small fry.

Sandpiper's Point, or affectionately "The Mekong Delta," approached, a spot where the mouth of a stream squashed out and emptied into the lake. The depth was perfect, and with the agitation of swirling water in the pools, action was nearly guaranteed.

ZZZZZ ... Preston's reel sang that magic melody. Somewhere we're stars. At the bend of his rod, more cameras lifted than at a Tiger Woods press conference. ZZZZZ tighten.

Does Your Meter Work?!

ZZZZZ tighten. Boating a nice pound and a bit brook trout brought smiles and waves from the latest pass of sightseers.

Duchess, Preston's Springer Spaniel that sat dispassionately between us, sniffed the fish, but the ducks, geese, and loons bobbing on the surface summoned her retriever instincts.

The weather, as usual, was a lottery. The cold in our bones couldn't break until the sun climbed over the peaks. Throughout the day, one minute we were sun tanning, and the next, cloud cover cut off all that nice scenery. Rain, sun, and snow toggled on a moment.

Trolling in as the sky clouded over and darkened, we caught and released a couple more until another nice one pounder co-operated, filling our limit of two each. Driving all night, fishing all day, and then making it home deserved decent keepers.

And decent is the understatement of the culinary century when dining on mountain-fresh trout. Their delicate scales cook off easily, leaving a tender skin and firm, sweet flesh that matches a sockeye salmon.

Patrick Binon, Executive Chef of Sardi's Restaurant in New York, advised that the meat speaks for itself. The key with trout is to not complicate it with too many spices. He stores his rainbows on ice and black pepper, then serves pan-fried fillets cooked with Portobello mushroom, spring onion, and a cabernet.

The dock arrived, we loaded up, showed off the whopper, and I took the wheel for the drive home. Past Medicine Lake, past some elk browsing in the ditch, east on Highway 16, and I set the cruise. ZZZZZ voiced my passenger ... asleep.

I replayed my battle again and again, recalling that sublime sensation, and I was hooked on Maligne Lake.

THE CITY OF CHAMPIONS IS MORE THAN JUST BLUSTERY <u>WINTER DAYS</u>

What Canadian city has the second largest Fringe Festival in the world, more parkland per square mile of urban sprawl than any other in North America, the world's largest shopping mall, the fastest growing economy in the country, The World Track and Field Championships this past summer, the second busiest Tony Roma's, only after Disneyland's, and is the service and jumping off point to a lake of crude oil many times greater than Saudi Arabia's?

It's a place called Edmonton.

Fur traders supplying The Hudson Bay Company arrived in the early nineteenth century to find the resident Indians disinclined to share their bounty. The North West Mounted Police, now the Royal Canadian Mounted Police (RCMP), built a fort on a curve of the North Saskatchewan River. As a favor to a clerk, the police force named the new settlement Edmonton, after the grungy East London community of the same name.

The federal government was anxious to settle the west. After a long public relations campaign in the United Kingdom, the well of fresh immigrants willing to pioneer a wide-open land dried up. Clifford Sifton, the Minister of the Interior, reached across Europe to the east, and found a fountain of talent perfect for a land with a reputation of hard winters. Slavs, such as Poles, Ukrainians, Hungarians and so on were tired of Russian domination, and easily settled into Western Canada. The New World resembled their roots - long winters, expansive prairie, loads of forest and pastureland. Best of all, no one was trying to kill them.

The population of Edmonton in 1892 was 700 hardy folks. It boomed during the Klondike gold rush near the turn of the century, and then grew to 9,000 by 1904; the year that Edmonton was incorporated as a city. When the Province of Alberta was founded in 1905 Edmonton was, by then, Alberta's largest community. Edmonton's size and central location made it the obvious selection to become the provincial capital.

Does Your Meter Work?!

In 1912, Edmonton on the north side of the river, and the town of Strathcona on the south, amalgamated into a combined population of over 53,000. The High Level Bridge was completed in 1913, linking the two sides and creating one of the city's better-known landmarks. The trading area of present-day Edmonton totals nearly a million.

From the Eastern European influence, Edmonton has earned the ignoble sobriquets Garlic City or Edmonchuk. It's also known as The City of Champions because of the past success of the Edmonton Eskimos football team and the Oilers hockey team of the NHL. You'll also hear Festival City because of a plethora of year round festivals and theater or River City because of the beautiful river valley and its developments. Edmonton is the capital of the most right wing government in Canada, and has a reputation of hard living, hard working, hard talking oil patch workers, truckloads of snoose-spittin' farmers, and a vocal opponent of federal gun registration laws. This image is in contrast to the sight of these same boors rubbing shoulders at the opera or sponsoring local art shows and neighborhood theater.

Even Edmonton's weather gets a bum rap. Because of Edmonton's geographical positioning, tucked in 200 miles behind the Rocky Mountains, moisture from prevailing warm winds from the Pacific Ocean gets wrung out over the mountains, leaving the humidity low and ever so pleasurable during the summer. The lack of moisture means Edmonton is generally spared the slush and ice of Eastern Canada. Everything comes with a price, so the dry air permits the temperatures to drop during winter. Two or three sessions per winter of 25 below comes with the territory. Clear and cold is the common forecast. Folks from coastal areas, especially the United Kingdom continually comment, "Even though it's cold, the sun shines and I'll make that trade." But anyone who's lived a winter or two soon comes to understand that Edmonton is undeserving of a reputation as a polar tundra outpost.

West Edmonton Mall is the largest shopping center in the world, built over three phases beginning in 1979. The same developers constructed the Mall of America in Bloomington, Minnesota, which overtook the crown for a few years. A recent addition of stores, movie theaters, a digital technology playground, and casino expansion pushed WEM back to the top. Millions of tourists travel to this, in effect, enclosed city each year to shop, ice skate, swim, eat, ride in submarines, watch dolphin shows, gamble, nightclub, and spend their money. Retailers enjoy a Christmas rush, of course, plus smile just as wide during July and August for the tourist season.

Whyte Avenue, the main street of defunct Strathcona, is now the trendy, Bohemian Greenwich Village of town. The Fringe Festival takes place in Old Strathcona for ten days in August, knitting its experimental and street theater with the coffee houses, nightclubs, eclectic shops, and street scenes. December is the time for the Ice on Whyte Festival, (www.osba.ab.ca) where 30 artists shape 100 blocks of ice into figurines. Not everyone is a fan of the neighborhood. Its growth has been criticized by the accumulation of late night drinking establishments (some claim a glut). Opponents assert booze subtracts from the tranquil, arty feel. A recent closing time riot fuelled by testosterone, alcohol, and questionable police strategies has galvanized anger coupled with cries of, "We've been telling you so!" by the residents. Late night noise during the summer has the populace on its own warpath, with no immediate resolution pending.

Besides The Fringe, the annual city extravaganza is dubbed Klondike Days, ten days in July of period costumes, hair plumage, and lace stockings for the ladies, and top hats, arm bands, and walking canes for the men. The International Street Performer's Festival and The Folk Festival have gained reputations among players as One Of The Ones to Attend If I Can Get Invited. The long weekend in August hosts Heritage Days, a party of multiculturalism that draws 350,000.

Edmonton is not nearly as busy as during the warm months. Labor Day sits as an unofficial deadline signifying the close of summer. Activities generally begin to move indoors. The Edmonton Symphony Orchestra, The Alberta Ballet, The Citadel Theatre, and

Winspear Concert Hall all start in on their new seasons. The John Janzen Nature Center (780 496 2939) celebrates fall with a new activity each week, and the Celebration of Nations Festival (www.geocities.com/cofnsociety) takes place the last week of September.

Gardeners gather their vegetables and farmers work long hours. Many of the nouveau riche take time off work to help out. Training camp opens for the NHL Oilers, which always sets the city on a buzz. Each year is filled with promise, although Edmontonians have *almost* moved on from the days of Gretzky, Messier, and Lowe. The most successful franchise of the Canadian Football League, the Eskimos, haven't missed the playoffs since 1972, and their yearly fate hangs heavily in the balance once the leaves begin to change color.

Candy Cane Lane is one of the city's most anticipated Christmas events. What started out as a few neighbors decorating their yards has turned into an annual event that employs virtually miles of cord and bushels of bulbs to light up approximately fifteen blocks of residential houses.

Massive, and we're talking *massive,* oil and gas deposits in Northern Alberta, headed by the oil sands of Fort MacMurray five hours north, plus successful provincial government after years of greed and nest-feathering, has turned Edmonton into the fastest growing city in Canada. Calgary, three hours south, toggles with Edmonton for the crown. Calgary has the corporate offices and management, and Edmonton the technical expertise and supply base. There's nothing like solid prices of crude and natural gas to keep the economy humming, and continue to put Ralph Klein's Progressive Conservatives in the seats of the legislature. Recent poorly planned deregulation of power put the premier in a hotter seat than he would like, but a spring election installed him with his largest mandate yet, garnering 74 of 83 seats.

Edmonton's greatest strength is for those raising a family – it's not a place to go blow off steam. Housing costs rank around twelfth in Canada, similar to Montreal without the prohibitive taxes. There are

Does Your Meter Work?!

tons of accessible, affordable, modern facilities: skating rinks, swimming pools, wide-open spaces, and traffic that neither chokes your nostrils or time. The streets are clean and wide. Facilities left over from the 1978 Commonwealth Games and 1982 Universiade put Edmonton a leg up on last August's World Track & Field Championships, the third largest sporting event going.

Younger singles find a lack of places to get into their own brands of excitement. Conservative puritans still retain a toehold on the politicians, evident in a recent bylaw banning rave dancing after 3 a.m. Nevertheless, Edmonton's strong job market, vibrant arts scene, and a small-town decency amid its rapid coming of age keeps skeptics around, or at least coming back after a trip to the not-so-greener other side of the fence.

<u>CULTURE SHOCK</u>

After two years, 22,000 miles, 62 beds, 13 countries, spider bites, feverish fevers, diarrhea, lactosis, halitosis, and more praying than a card-carrying agnostic is comfortable with, I was back in North America from Asia. I had landed in San Francisco airport and wondered how U.S. customs would accept my appearance and full passport of stamps.

Immigration slapped down a stamp without a hitch and I moved to the bag-check area. The agent there instructed me to pass by two others who had formed a line and go to the next officer.

The second-in-line didn't take kindly to my advancing quicker than he, and informed me "to get to the back of the bus." Overcoming jet lag requires burning concentration and I was sure I had heard the initial instructions correctly. Timidly, I returned to the officer and asked for a repeat.

"Go around those two people in Aisle 3, and see the agent in Aisle 4, like I told you last time," he snorted.

"That's what I thought you said," I muttered insecurely to myself.

"Then why did you come back?"

"This guy in Aisle 3 told me to get behind him," I tattled.

"WHO TOLD YOU TO DO THAT?!" he bellowed, his eyes like a poacher's jacklight.

Mr. Back Of The Bus, with round professor glasses and a campus look, put up his hand and volunteered his position with ersatz courage. The officer, hands on his hips, stood over the outgunned mouthpiece, and listened in silence. Then I heard,

"ARE YOU GETTING SMART WITH ME, BOY? MR. CARMEN, I WANT THIS MAN OVER AT 6-B!"

Mr. Carmen was another officer standing about, probably a supervisor of some sort.

"You want him over at 6-B?" Mr. Carmen asked with a wisp of uncertainty.

"Yes, Mr. Carmen, 6-B!" enunciated with special emphasis, like part of a code.

Each player strode confidently to the other side of the inspection area behind a wall. I muttered again, this time a silent prayer for the loudmouth, then put my money on The Law. Who knows how long Captain Campus endured at 6-B and what remained of him and his belongings. He broke Rule 1-A in The United States: Don't piss off the good ol' boys.

I sailed through the remainder of Customs and was now officially, legally on North American soil.

Helpful airport workers directed me to a San Francisco bus stop. My jet lag continued to ransack my ability to remember what the previous person had explained so instead I just asked whoever next came along. They all understood and fielded my questions.

In San Francisco, I stopped three different people on the street to ask directions to the bus depot and received a response in English. Storefronts advertised in English. The information board at the bus depot read in English and I found my own way without asking for help.

The next bus out to Sacramento left in half an hour. The announcement, in English, directed me exactly to my boarding area. The patient bus waited precisely where promised.

The uniformed bus driver made his way down the aisle and said, "Tickets, tickets." Lifting my head to see his face, I watched and understood those words leave his lips. I was conditioned to, and instinctively expected, either a funny stare or hand-signs, or both, from a bus employee in flip-flops and a muscle shirt while I sweated among the fragrances of chickens and armpits. As a test to verify this dream, I asked the trip's duration and the driver's response of "about two hours" was both believable and understood, not simply said because any answer is better than no answer at all.

Leaning back in that big, ol' comfortable seat, the real relief swimming through my veins was like coming out of a big sleep, awakening the old Jim I used to know. Like the blind man who gets a lucky rap on the head, blinks his eyes, maybe rubs them a bit, then shouts, "I can see, I CAN SEE!" I could feel the shackles melting away. I was no longer feeling my way around in the dark, no longer struggling for suspect information, no longer riddled with tension, unsure if I was on the correct bus, boat, ferry, train, car, or yak for that matter. Or if the time -- or even date -- of departure was accurate.

Does Your Meter Work?!

We wheeled into Sacramento right on time. It was clean, cool, fresh, uncrowded, modern, and had the qualities of home. By now, I wanted a place to lay my head. A few seedy hotels seemed like too much money. In the travel section of a book store in a nearby mall, I scrawled on my hand the address of the local youth hostel from a guide book, asked someone outside for the abode's location, and walked there in ten minutes.

It was a beautifully refurbished old house with oak floors and a grand twisting staircase leading upstairs to the rooms. The exceedingly friendly staff found me a bed.

While waiting to check in, I watched a peculiar game of baseball, odd because most players were southpaws. I adjusted to the oddity, and then Robbie Alomar lined one to center. A switch hitter nailing one up the middle was normal, but then he took off toward third base rather than first. A right-handed Ken Griffey Jr. easily fielded the one-hopper and tossed it to a shortstop that covered from the wrong side of second. It looked very much like baseball, everyone ran in the same directions, played the same rules, everyone's play was meshing, except backwards. If not backwards, then at least the other way around. Just when I felt comfortable with the changes, a hit took place that could have been executed within either game, the proper one or this unusual one. I juggled the anomalies, and had to select which game the normalcy belonged to. Living in Asia is like watching baseball in a mirror.

Bright fluorescent lights above a large mirror illuminated the magnificent bathroom. Linoleum floors squeaked under my bare feet. Inside a cabinet, pails, glass cleaner, SOS pads, sink and toilet cleaner, mops, rags, you name it, signified "CLEAN!" The bouquet of Pine-Sol gladdened my nostrils. The spanking antiseptic environment encouraged a deep breath in and out. I comprehended further how much and how long my guard had been up.

Without needing to concentrate on completely spitting out the rinse water, I brushed my teeth in peace. I even swallowed a little. I never knew a shower to be gorgeous but this one had separate handles for hot and cold and a third to divert the water from the spout to the head. No kidding, Pavlovian drool moistened my mouth while I adjusted the temperature to be juuuuust right.

Does Your Meter Work?!

Drying off, a trickle of water collecting from my hair ran down my back. I autonomically flinched, believing the tickle must be an insect, then let up. That big, bright beautiful mirror confirmed what I already knew, but I twisted to look anyway. I stared into my own eyes, welcoming and, at the same time, preparing for culture shock. I wasn't home yet, but America was closer to Canada than I'd been in two years. I still wasn't sure who that was in the mirror.

The long travel had stifled hunger, thirst, and exploration. Only my bed called. Under a quilt I did slip my weary carcass and felt my body's warmth replace the evening's cool, fresh air; a pleasant divergence to the equatorial sleeping routine of laying nude, uncovered in the tropical heat wishing I had more clothes to take off.

My unadjusted biological clock turned and tossed me the entire night. By 6 a.m., hunger still hadn't arrived but the recollection of REAL BACON AND EGGS proved too strong, pulling me from the boredom of pursuing sleep that had no chance of capture.

An absence of greasy spoons in the immediate area meant my tonic of bacon and eggs would have to wait. This was California with coffee shops crowing low fat and whole bran and sugarless and decaf latte. Sacrilegious choices for someone breakfast-shopping more in the over-due over-indulgence line.

With the coffees lined up and, scratching my skull, I tried to make a decision. Irish Cream, Medium Roast, Mocha-Java Partial Decaf, French Dark.

"Could I just have a lousy cup of coffee?" I contemplated out loud.

The girl saw me looking over the menu and smiled empathetically.

"We don't have lousy coffee...What can I get you?"

"I just want a plain old, garden variety, house dressing cup of coffee."

"Colombian light roast is probably what you want."
"Sold."

"Would you like something to eat this morning?" she sang.
"Probably...hang on a sec."

Does Your Meter Work?!

I recoiled again. Such colloquial English should shape a look of incomprehension on her face. She stood back patiently with the same face. I smiled inside.

Then my breakfast presented itself. I pointed through the glass casing like a little boy chooses his puppy at the pet store. It was a cinnamon bun, as big as my hand, its layers racing around and around, the cinnamon bulging out between the pastry's lines interrupted by great, big raisin speed bumps. Pit-stopped on a bench outside, I unwrapped the tightly wound wraps, pulled apart sizable chunks, and jammed them into my mouth. Gulps of coffee washed down each chew. The icing cascaded off my forefinger, then middle finger, ring finger, and finally my pinky. I left the sticky goo on until the bun was done, then, as dessert, I lapped up the icing between my digits.

I found a payphone and called my friends, which is why I had boogied to Sacramento, by the by. They zipped over immediately and picked me up. Our conversations continued with the state of world affairs and various other offshoots of stand-up philosophy. I felt a major sense of accomplishment. Traveling à la carte provides an up close and personal education, something not attainable from text books, not fully grasped from TV, and only as good as a story-teller is capable in his craft. Staying in five-star resorts, hopping onto a tour bus for glimpses of the streets, then back to the hotel for a rubdown and cognac is a misleading fraction of the story. Tourists are sheltered by the glass between the inside of the bus and the truth that is occurring down below, the sweat and spit of everyday life. Table d'hôte or set-menu travel is a cartoon for the viewer, not the real deal.

I lapped up each moment like a long lost cat that has found its way back. Still, I couldn't stay forever. The thought of my mother's mushroomed pork chops, my Auntie Shirley's stew with dumplings, and my spaghetti sauce was dragging me away from Sacramento.

Three days later, the next stop was Vancouver. Cousin Randy's familiar teal, short-box Chevy pulled up at Arrivals Loading, and he bounced out of the cab. I threw my clothes-filled duffel bag at him like a medicine ball and he tossed it into the back. We had a nice, big family hug and shared the same thought simultaneously.

Does Your Meter Work?!

"HAS IT BEEN TWO YEARS OUT OF THE COUNTRY!?"
We strolled along English Bay with Colin and Mary, two more friends, trying to keep pace with their two young kids, a lost cause if I ever saw one. I begged for that energy, especially in India.

A Canadian flag flew over an apartment -- it started to hit me where I was. Clean streets ran through a busy commercial area. The odd cigarette butt seemed to jump up and down, hopelessly lost, yelling, "Pick me up!" The air didn't stink. I wasn't sweating. I strolled slowly because of relaxation, not perspiration-phobia. Canadian coins jingled in my pocket -- I didn't have to learn another currency on sight. A purple ten note, a blue fiver. We cruised into a shop and I pulled out a green bill, unwittingly aware of two things. One, it was a twenty and two, it would be enough for our drinks. Its value had relevance. A casual glance recognized the mixture of currency the clerk handed back. I knew at once it was the correct change.

Answers to my questions regarding hockey were current and informed. The Canucks could still be better, the Oilers were too young but showed promise, and the Rangers spent too much on salaries.

During our conversations, relaxed and informal, I knew exactly who I gabbed with, how many brothers and sisters they had, all their births, deaths, and marriages. My comrades weren't other travelers whose immediate histories and/or futures was the only topic of conversation.

Leashed dogs sat together sociably without copulating or snarling or fighting over food. Smells were aromas: soap, fresh coffee, fresh bread, fresh air. The smells were not odors: shit, burnt woks, my feet. The only clutter on the sidewalks was tables and chairs -- placed out of the way. Walking by, I heard and understood snippets of others' conversations. A car horn honked. Heads turned to evaluate the seriousness of the infraction to merit a horn. To keep up to the horns in Asia, we'd all look like Linda Blair in The Exorcist. No one screamed incomprehensible noises. No one stared. Hell, this was easy!

Next was the big day, home to Edmonton. The unending checkerboard pattern of the western Canadian prairie drew closer and closer until touchdown.

Does Your Meter Work?!

During the drive into the city, I saw my friend Ken's bagel shop still the same. All the big box stores were intact, a few new names, same hotels, same street names. My home, the denominator in my equation, which had changed little, if at all, was still here. I was the numerator with a dramatically changed value.

The shuttle bus from the airport stopped at the downtown Westin Hotel and I hauled my things onto the ramp. The afternoon air was fresh, dry, and mild. The smell of the sap running in the trees and pollen floating was sweet, as though God had sprinkled sugar in the air. In the back of a waiting taxi, I gave the address to my mother's house. The cabby threw it in drive then stopped for oncoming traffic. A sparrow landed in a tree, then skittered from branch to branch, like I had hitchhiked from Brunei to Bangkok, branch to branch, car to car, town to town. I felt united with him, not envious of his freedom. He's lucky to be a songbird in Canada rather than a rooster in the Philippines. The traffic cleared. The cabby pulled onto the street and turned his meter on.

<u>MARIAN HOSSA</u>

"Do you know Marian Hossa?" asked my friend Ab a few years back. Ab's one of those guys you'd go to war with, no knees left from installing floors ("Journeyman Floor Mechanic" he says with a laugh"), loves his kids, first guy out with his money, you know the type. We've been friends for the past quarter century- attended all the same births, deaths, and marriages. Jerry Seinfeld owes royalties to our gang.

"Yeah, he's that rookie with Ottawa. He's gonna be a star. He is already, in fact," I replied, faking my knowledge more than I'd like.

"Is he? I don't know him. Christy (Ab's daughter) met him last weekend at that club for kids, Barry T's. The Senators were in town playing the Oilers, and he started talking with her."

Little wonder, with Christy's' head of hair, a pair of back pockets that refuse to quit, and a decorous demeanor. She'd be the Belle of the Bar wherever she goes. Lucky for her she didn't take after the old man.

"Oh, yeah? Did she like him?"

"She says he's a nice guy. He's been calling her almost everyday, he leaves messages for her. He seems like a nice kid…shy…it's cute."

"It's funny, these sports stars are such big heroes, lots of money, they seem bigger than life itself, but they're chasing girls and bamboozled by all the same confusions everyone else their age is."

Since then, Cupid has been on his game, and Christy and Marian have become a couple, with Christy traveling back and forth to Ottawa, and around the world. Ab's kept us current with their comings and goings, always with a shrug, unassuming to any celebrity that may be involved. I had even of late helped them find a Slovakian teacher for Christy.

Does Your Meter Work?!

Recently, Ab and I played a game of hockey in our beer league, and naturally, went for beers afterwards. Highlights of Marian's four-goal game, each of the spectacular sort, was the buzz on the myriad TV sets surrounding us.

"How're Christy and Marian, Ab?"

"Good. Christy went to Ottawa for awhile, but she's coming home next week."

The next week after our game, we're in a different bar, same pulled muscles though, same star of the show on all the TV's. Highlights revealed another multi-goal game by our hero.

"Geez, Ab, he skates like his future old-man-in-law. What's up with your kid? Has she paid off your mortgage yet?"

"Christy's coming home tonight. David (her brother) is picking her up at the airport as we speak."

Fast-forward a few nights: I am now working my weekend job, driving a cab, and business is the grunts. I'm bored rigid, and feeling awfully sorry for myself. I'm parked in front of a nightclub around 2 a.m. with doors locked and ready to refuse any drunken boneheads from barreling into my cab when a single male appears outside the doorway, talking on his cell phone.

"Looks like, nah, well, maybe, yeah, could be Marian Hossa," I find myself thinking. Business has been so bad, I was ready to see Liz Manley toe-loop across the frozen parking lot and throw an elbow at Dave Keon.

Continuing to speak into his phone, this young, fit man in casual, baggy clothes walks up to the passenger-side rear door of my hack-for-always-hire and before I know it, he's pulling on the door handle. I hit open because a broke cab driver always gives in, and the bloke has climbed right in. At least he looks, smells, and sounds sober, whoever he is, and he's not yet questioned the marital status of my parents at my birth. Young, boozed-up males late at night, snow falling, temperature in the minus region, just want in, decorum be damned. They stick cabbies in the basement suite on society's outhouse.

The shadows are dark, but I still can't help but notice that my customer looks more and more like the TV pictures of Mrs. Hossa's son without the pads and visor. Then his face moves into a beam of light just as I hear his Slavic accent for the first time.

"Okie, okie, vot's you address, then?" he speaks into the phone.

"Geezuz, it IS Marian Hossa!"

Parroting to me what he is hearing over the phone, he reports as clearly as an imported bell to my reddened ears, "one-five-one…" then he is waiting for the next clump of numbers.

I need no further proof: A Hundred and Fifty-First Avenue! Ab's house and all his great floors! I turn more to face him and inquire in almost professional manner, "You, er, want to go to Christy's house?"

"Huh," he gulps incredulously.

"Do you want to go to Christy's house?" I ask, now that I'm practically famous, in a reassured, modestly cocky tone in my voice. You're on MY home ice now, pal.

"You know Christy…?" His new response is delivered in precisely equal but disbelieving proportion to that of my own newly mined courage.

"UH-huh…"

"My cab driver knows you," Marian vacantly says into the phone. "Who are you, sir, Christy wants to know?"

"I'm a friend of her dad's."

Does Your Meter Work?!

He repeats my response, and then asks with a private eye's wariness, a testing question for a possible interloper on the fame path, "Then what's his name?"

"Tell her 'Your dad is Ab…your brother is David…'"

"OK, but then who are you?"

"I'm Jim."

"Now she knows. So you know where we're going?"

"I know exactly."

"I'll see you soon," Romeo promises his Juliet. "Ciao."

At points during the 20-minute ride, I'm silently juggling whether to charge Marian or not. I mean, we're practically family! But then, these guys don't get paid enough; road trip per diem's for food, cabs, bail etc. run around 70 dollars a day, best I can figure. But it's Senator owner Rod Bryden's money in the end. Everything I hear way out west here, Rod's a good guy, but not about to miss a meal in spite of the Senator's money woes, so greed supersedes self-sacrifice as we pull onto a Hundred and Fifty-First Avenue and park in front of Ab's house.

I hit the "end trip" button and point to the damage. Marian's fare is 24 bucks and change, which he pays with a 50 from a jumble of bills, and asks for 20 back, no receipt. Odd for a guy from Ottawa.

"Thanks for the tip, Marian, maybe we'll see you for a bar-b-que in the summer," I think to myself, as David, standing in the front window with his shirt off, watches his darned-near brother-in-law walk up and into the house.

The Senators had beaten Calgary that night, and afterwards the team had flown into Edmonton. Number 18 had taken a cab to the club along with three teammates, and waited for the siren call of his love, her proud father, and somewhat clothed brother, whom were driving back to Edmonton after the game.

Marian Hossa. A modest young hockey superstar with great hands, speed to burn, big tips, and spot-on taste in women.

At the Tim Horton's, I order coffee, but I'm already revved. But there's nobody to talk to, even the waitress is from a country where hockey is untranslatable. I recall seeing Guy LaFleur and his wife (probably) walking down the street in London. "Hey…Guy LaFleur!" I called to him in admiration. He nodded, nearly smiled, but what Brit at the pub later could care of my sighting. Just like now. What good is coming in touch with Marian Hossa if it has to stay his and my little secret? Three a.m. and no one to tell. The young toughs, 3.5 sails to the ice fog, don't even look so thuggish. Hell, I'll go into the corner with them now.

I better call Ab.

Does Your Meter Work?!

Dear Reader,

Whew…you made it. That's all there is, there ain't no more. Whether you read the whole thing in one sitting on a 24-hour bus trip perhaps, or your journey took 44 months, as in one story a month while the book sat on your night table between readings, without an audience my book contains no value, so thank you so much for providing that value by reading it.

But don't take it from me. Who says you can't go to these places and touch, taste, see, hear, and smell them for yourself rather than living vicariously through another's tales? Traveling won't lead to fame and fortune, but it nourishes and fertilizes ones soul. Travel is an entity completely unto itself, and so are you. Combining the two is one of life's great gifts.

The toughest part is getting on the plane…

Thanks again.

Jim Soliski

Does Your Meter Work?!

Jim Soliski was born on a Friday the 13th in 1961 and grew up in Evansburg, Alberta, Canada, a small farming community where he lived a Huckleberry Finn childhood. He speaks a rusted-out French, enough Ukrainian to make his Baba laugh out loud, and adequate Mandarin and Spanish to get his face slapped. He likes to play fastball, hockey and golf, go hunting and fishing, take pictures, cook, and he constantly schemes his next trip.

His stories have been published in the following:

Alexandria Journal; American Express Dreamscapes; Arlington Journal; BabylonTravel.com; Barrie Examiner; Boston Globe; Brantford Expositor; Calgary Herald; Calgary Straight; Charlotte Leader; Chicago Tribune; Cornwall Standard Freeholder; Cusco Weekly (Peru); Daily Journal; Dirty Trails Traveler; Echo Magazine; Edmonton Journal; Edmonton Sun; Ex-Pat Magazine (Hong Kong); Fairfax Journal; Florida Times-Union; Georgia Straight; Globe and Mail; Jetsetliving.com; Kingston Whig-Standard; Montgomery Journal; Montreal Gazette; Naples Daily News; National Post; New Glasgow Evening News; Niagara Falls Review; OC (Orange County) Weekly; Outpost Magazine; Phoenix News; Prairie Dog; Prince George Citizen; Prince George's Journal; Providence Journal; St. Catherines Standard; St. Petersburg Times; San Francisco Examiner; SEE Magazine; Seen.com; Signspotting; Spokane News & Review; Sunday Mercury (U.K.); Transitions Abroad; Travelers' Tales; TravelMag.co.uk; Truro Daily News; Vancouver Sun; Victoria Times-Colonist; Vue Weekly